GA... K. MEYER

Ibiza Travel Guide 2023

*Everything You Need to Know About Visiting Ibiza,
including When to Go, What to Do, and Where to Stay
with Essential Tips for First Timers*

First edition

This book was professionally typeset on Reedsy.
Find out more at reedsy.com

Contents

Welcome to Ibiza

I felt the warm wind of Ibiza embrace me as soon as I walked out of the airport. I couldn't wait to see the vibrant nightlife and beautiful beaches. I was very excited to see Ibiza and its party scene since I'd heard so much about it.

I spent my first day in Ibiza exploring the island and meeting locals. I strolled along the cobblestone lanes, enjoying the whitewashed homes and the flowers that ornamented them. As I wandered, I couldn't help but notice the kind people who greeted me with warm smiles and welcoming gestures.

I came into a little bar one evening and decided to pop in for a drink. I sat at the bar and began up a chat with the bartender, a friendly Ibicenco keen to impart his local expertise. He advised me on the best places to party as well as the hidden gems that most visitors miss.

The following day, I took his advice and went to a secluded beach he had suggested. Although it took some work, it was worthwhile. The beach was beautiful, with crystal blue water and silky sand that felt like velvet under my feet. I was sitting in the sun when I observed a bunch of Indians nearby singing and dancing. I was first hesitant to approach them, but I soon found myself joining in on their fun.

That night, I went to one of the clubs suggested by the bartender. The music was pulsing, and the mood was charged. I danced and drank with the indigenous people, feeling as if I were one of them.

The days after that were a flurry of sun, beach, and pleasure. I met a lot of lovely individuals and had a lot of memorable experiences. I went cliff diving with the locals, discovered secret coves, and even went on a sunset boat cruise.

I also visited a local market, where I saw some of the island's traditional crafts and sampled some of the delectable native vegetables. The market was humming with activity, with vendors selling everything from handmade pottery to fresh seafood.

As my time in Ibiza came to an end, I was overcome with sadness. I didn't want to leave this lovely island or the people who had made it seem like home to me. But I knew I'd never forget my time in Ibiza or the memories I'd built there.

On my last night in Ibiza, I returned to the neighborhood pub where I had met the friendly bartender. He welcomed me with a warm grin and an embrace, and we spoke about my incredible adventures on the island. As I made my way back to my hotel, I couldn't help but be thankful for the incredible experience I'd just had. Ibiza and its inhabitants had genuinely stolen my heart, and I knew this gorgeous island will always have a special place in my heart.

Introduction to Ibiza

Ibiza is a stunning island in Spain's Balearic archipelago known for its breathtaking natural beauty, vibrant nightlife, and affluent lifestyle. It is situated in the western Mediterranean Sea and is the third largest of the Balearic Islands, after Mallorca and Menorca. Because of its moderate temperature, crystal-clear oceans, and enough sunshine, Ibiza is a popular destination for travelers from all over the world searching for a nice and memorable holiday experience.

Ibiza has a long history, having been inhabited by the Phoenicians, Greeks, and Romans. It was also an important hub for the Mediterranean pirate trade throughout the Middle Ages. Ibiza is now known for its eclectic culture, which draws influences from all around the world. Because of its unique combination of historic Spanish culture, current European lifestyles, and foreign influences, the island is a fascinating vacation.

One of Ibiza's main draws is its amazing natural beauty. The scenery on the island includes everything from rocky coves and sandy beaches to undulating hills and towering mountains. The island's coastline is particularly well-known for its crystal-clear oceans and spectacular sunsets, which attract visitors from all over the world. The island's beaches are also well-known for their beauty and variety, ranging from secret coves to hectic party areas. The most popular beaches on the island are Playa d'en Bossa, Cala Comte, and Ses Salines.

Another major lure is Ibiza's thriving nightlife. The island is famous for its clubs, taverns, and parties, which draw visitors from all over the world. The island's nightlife industry is particularly well-known for its electronic music, which has become synonymous with Ibiza's party culture. The clubs and bars on the island remain open late, with several well-known DJs and performers performing regularly. Some of the most well-known clubs on the island include Amnesia, Pacha, and Ushuaa.

Ibiza also boasts a strong food and drink culture, with a wide range of culinary experiences accessible. The food on the island is inspired by civilizations all around the world, with a concentration on fresh fish and local goods. Paella, seafood stews, and grilled fish are among the island's most popular dishes. The island is also famous for its wine, with several local vineyards producing superb red and white wines.

Ibiza has a lot to offer those seeking a more calm and cultural experience as well. Dalt Vila, Ibiza's old village and a UNESCO World Heritage Site, is one of the island's most significant sites. The village is distinguished by winding cobblestone streets, historic buildings, and stunning views of the Mediterranean Sea. On the island, there are also museums, art galleries, and cultural events that emphasize the island's rich history and cultural past.

Geography and Climate

Ibiza is a lovely island in the Balearic Sea in the Mediterranean. The Spanish island is famous for its stunning beaches, active nightlife, and cultural heritage. Ibiza has a total land area of 571.6 square kilometers and a 210-kilometer coastline.

The geography of the island is varied, with rugged hills, limestone cliffs, and little bays. Sa Talaia is the highest peak on the island, rising 475 meters above sea level. Ibiza's scenery is dotted with almond trees, olive orchards, and pine woods.

The island has a Mediterranean climate with warm summers and moderate winters. The average temperature of Ibiza ranges from 10°C in the winter to 30°C in the summer. Every year, the island receives over 300 days of sunshine, making it an ideal destination for sunbathers.

The many little islands that ring the main island are one of Ibiza's most distinguishing features. Because of their secluded beaches and crystal-clear oceans, these tiny islands, which include Es Vedra, Tagomago, and S'Espartar, are popular with vacationers.

Ibiza also includes several natural parks and protected areas, which showcase the island's rich biodiversity. The Ses Salines Natural Park, located in the south of the island, is a UNESCO World Heritage Site that is home to a variety of avian and marine life.

The island's climate is heavily influenced by its location in the Mediterranean. Ibiza's summers are scorching, but the winters are mild, with temperatures seldom dropping below freezing. The island is a well-liked tourist destination for visitors from all over the globe because to its pleasant temperature, gorgeous beaches, and exciting nightlife.

Ibiza's coastline is dotted with little bays, coves, and beaches surrounded by cliffs and pine trees. The beaches on the island are well known for their clean waters and fine sand. Some of the most popular beaches on the island include Cala d'Hort, Cala Comte, and Talamanca.

Despite its small size, Ibiza's geography is quite diverse, with something for every kind of traveler. With its rocky hills and limestone cliffs, peaceful beaches, and natural parks, the island is a true nature lover's paradise.

The island's geography has also had a profound impact on the development of its cultural history. Ibiza has been inhabited since antiquity, and its unique geography has given the island an important strategic location for trade and defense.

The island's climate has also influenced its traditional architecture, which has whitewashed buildings with low roofs and shaded courtyards to keep cool during the scorching summer months. The Mediterranean climate has also had a significant impact on the island's traditional food, which emphasizes fresh fish, olive oil, and local goods.

Ethnicity and Culture in Ibiza

Ibiza, a tiny Spanish island in the Mediterranean Sea, is a popular destination for visitors from all over the globe. The island's cultural milieu is diverse and rich, blending European and North African cultures. The population of the island is ethnically varied, with many people coming from Spain, Italy, and North Africa.

Ibiza has a rich history of cultural diversity, with several civilizations dominating the island throughout the centuries. Phoenicians, Carthaginians, Romans, and Arabs all left their mark on Ibiza's culture, architecture, and traditions.

The cultural environment of Ibiza is known for its distinct blend of traditional Spanish culture and current European influences. The architecture, food, and language of the island reflect its Spanish heritage, with Spanish being the most widely spoken language on the island.

Ibiza, on the other hand, is known for its vibrant and diverse nightlife, with electronic music playing a significant role in the island's party scene. This aspect of Ibiza's culture has drawn people from all over the world, giving the island a truly global atmosphere.

Ibiza has a diverse ethnic population, including residents of Spanish, Italian, North African, and other European roots. Because of its geographical location, the island has become a melting pot of cultures and practices, with each group contributing to the island's own cultural identity.

Ibiza is known for its relaxed and calm culture, with a focus on enjoying life's simple pleasures. The island's population is kind and welcoming, with a strong sense of community. The island's natural beauty and pleasant environment make it ideal for outdoor activities like hiking, swimming, and sunbathing.

The island's gastronomic culture is also an essential aspect of its cultural milieu. The island's cuisine is a fusion of Spanish, Mediterranean, and North African flavors, with fresh seafood featuring prominently in many dishes. The island's food is simple yet delicious, with a focus on using fresh, locally sourced products.

The Feast of Saint John, held every year on June 24th, is one of Ibiza's most prominent cultural festivals. The celebration of the summer solstice includes bonfires, fireworks, and traditional dancing. It is a period when the island's cultural legacy is celebrated.

Music culture is another essential aspect of the island's cultural identity. Some of the world's most famous clubs, such as Pacha, Amnesia, and Ushuaa, can be found in Ibiza. The nightlife on the island attracts some of the world's most famous DJs and music enthusiasts, with electronic dance music dominating the clubs.

Ibiza's music scene has had a significant influence on the island's cultural environment, with the island's club culture impacting music cultures throughout the world. Many notable DJs and producers have been influenced by Ibiza's music scene, and the island is considered a haven for enthusiasts of electronic music.

Another major cultural aspect of Ibiza is its traditional crafts. Crafts on the island have a long history, with traditional skills passed down from generation to generation. Ceramics, basket weaving, and embroidery are among the island's traditional crafts.

Crafts are a significant element of Ibiza's cultural past, with many local artisans conserving traditional techniques. Tourists like the island's crafts as well, with many going home with homemade presents from their Ibiza holidays.

Historical background of Ibiza

Ibiza has a fascinating history that dates back thousands of years. In this guide, we will look at the history of Ibiza, from its early colonies to its current status as a popular tourist destination.

Ibiza has been inhabited since prehistoric times, with traces of Bronze Age human habitation. The earliest documented residents were the Phoenicians, who established a commercial port on the island in the 7th century BCE. In the fifth century BCE, the Carthaginians conquered the island and utilized it as a base for their naval operations in the western Mediterranean.

In the second century BCE, the Romans conquered Ibiza and incorporated it into their empire. During this time, the island became a center for agriculture and commerce, with salt manufacturing being one of its main industries. The Romans also built several important structures on the island, including a network of roads, aqueducts, and public buildings.

After the Roman Empire fell, Ibiza was governed by the Vandals, then the Byzantines, and lastly the Moors. During the Moorish dominion, which lasted from the seventh through the twelfth century, the island saw tremendous growth and development. Citrus fruits, rice, and sugar cane were all brought by the Moors as new agricultural methods and crops. They also built other major structures on the island, like the Almudaina Castle in Ibiza Town.

In the 13th century, the Catalan-Aragonese Crown, which included the neighboring island of Mallorca, conquered Ibiza. On the island, the Crown established a feudal system, with vast estates governed by "senyors" who collected taxes from the peasants who cultivated the land. During this time, the island became an important center for salt production, which was shipped to other parts of Europe.

In the 16th century, Ibiza was often raided by pirates enticed by the island's strategic location and wealth. In response, the islanders built defensive structures like watchtowers and fortified churches. Many of these structures may still be seen on the island today, and many of them have been converted into museums or cultural institutes.

In the 18th century, the Bourbon monarchy took over Ibiza, bringing an era of modernity and development to the island. To boost the island's economy and infrastructure, the monarchy abolished the feudal system and imposed new laws and regulations. During this time, Ibiza also became an important commercial and business center, with the port of Ibiza Town serving as a hub for ships traveling between Spain and other parts of Europe.

Ibiza had tremendous growth and development as a result of the tourist industry during the twentieth century. In the 1960s and 1970s, the island became popular among young people seeking sun, beach, and nightlife. As a consequence, a bustling club scene developed, with many well-known DJs and bands performing at venues like Pacha and Amnesia. Ibiza is still one of Europe's most popular tourist destinations, attracting millions of visitors each year with its beautiful beaches, vibrant nightlife, and rich cultural heritage.

Why visit Ibiza?

I biza, the third biggest island in the Balearic Islands, is famous for its beautiful beaches, vibrant nightlife, and attractive scenery. It's no wonder that Ibiza has become one of the world's most popular tourist destinations, with its colorful energy and inviting attitude. Here are the top eleven reasons to visit Ibiza.

1. Beautiful Beaches: Ibiza offers some of the world's most gorgeous beaches. There is something for everyone, with over 80 beaches to pick from. Ibiza offers everything, whether you want a hidden cove or a vibrant beach with loads of activities. Cala Bassa, Playa d'en Bossa, and Cala Jondal are among the most popular beaches.
2. Amazing Nightlife: Ibiza is well-known for its fantastic nightlife. You'll have a great night out with world-famous nightclubs like Pacha, Amnesia, and Ushuaa. Ibiza features a club for every musical taste, whether it's techno, house, or hip-hop.
3. Delicious food: Ibiza is home to some of the world's top restaurants. Ibiza's cuisine is both tasty and healthful, thanks to a concentration on fresh, local products. There is something for every appetite, from classic Spanish tapas to foreign food.
4. Spectacular Sunsets:Sunsets are spectacular in Ibiza, and watching them is a very wonderful experience. There are several locations in Ibiza to enjoy a spectacular sunset, from the beaches to the hills. Cafe del Mar is the most popular sunset site, where you may sip a drink while watching the sunset.

5. Outdoor Recreation: Ibiza has lots to offer in terms of adventure. There are several outdoor activities to keep you engaged, ranging from hiking and cycling to water sports and diving. The craggy shoreline and crystal-clear seas of the island make it an ideal location for water sports aficionados.

6. A thriving cultural heritage: Ibiza has a long cultural history dating back thousands of years. Ibiza has a wonderful history that is just waiting to be unearthed, ranging from Phoenician colonies through the hippy movement of the 1960s and 1970s. A variety of museums and galleries on the island also display the island's cultural past.

7. Lovely countryside: While Ibiza is famous for its beaches and nightlife, the island's hinterland is as stunning. The environment of Ibiza has a lot to offer, from rolling hills to charming towns. The island also has many environmental reserves and parks that are ideal for hiking and cycling.

8. Relaxation: Ibiza is the ideal spot for unwinding and relaxing. You may escape the rush and bustle of daily life and recharge your batteries in its relaxed environment and serene surroundings. Ibiza offers everything you need to relax, whether you want to indulge in a spa treatment or just lounge on the beach.

9. Shopping and Fashion: Ibiza is well-known for its fashion and shopping. Ibiza has something for everyone, from high-end stores to bohemian markets. The island also has several local designers that manufacture one-of-a-kind and fashionable apparel that you won't find anyplace else.

10. Sports and Fitness: If you like working out, Ibiza has a lot to offer. There are several exercise alternatives available, ranging from yoga and Pilates to personal training and boot camps. There are also a lot of sporting facilities on the island, such as tennis courts, golf courses, and football fields.

11. Festivals and Special Events: Throughout the year, Ibiza hosts a variety of festivals and events. There is always something going on in Ibiza, from the International Music Summit in May to the closing celebrations in September. The island is particularly well-known for its annual Ibiza Carnival, held in February, and a colorful celebration of the island's

history and traditions.

Chapter 1: Planning Your Trip to Ibiza

I t may be difficult to plan a trip to Ibiza, particularly if it is your first time there. With a little planning and preparation, you can guarantee that your vacation to Ibiza is one you will never forget.

The first step in organizing an Ibiza vacation is to choose a date. Summer is the busiest season on the island, with the peak season lasting from June through August. Travel during the shoulder season in May, September, or October for a more relaxed experience.

After you've settled on a date, the following step is to reserve your lodging. Ibiza has hotels to suit all budgets, from luxury resorts to low-cost hostels. It is important to pick where you wish to stay on the island since each location provides a distinct experience. If you prefer a lively nightlife scene, stay in Ibiza Town or San Antonio, for example.

Next, decide what you want to accomplish throughout your vacation. Ibiza is well-known for its nightlife, but there is still much to do during the day. Ibiza has something for everyone, from seeing ancient sights like Dalt Vila to exploring the island's beautiful beaches.

If you want to experience the island's famed nightlife, do some research on the key clubs and events. Ibiza is home to some of the world's most well-known clubs, including Pacha and Amnesia, which draw world-renowned DJs and partygoers from all over the globe.

Don't forget about transportation while organizing your vacation. Despite the island's modest size, getting about without a vehicle or scooter may be challenging. To get about the island, consider hiring a car or using public transit.

Finally, don't forget to plan your vacation thoroughly. Because the weather in Ibiza is pleasant and bright, carry lots of sunscreen and light clothes. If you wish to visit the island's beaches, bring a swimsuit and a beach towel.

The best time to visit

Millions of travelers visit Ibiza each year to experience its distinct atmosphere and enjoy its various attractions. However, if you want to make the most of your vacation to Ibiza, you must travel at the correct time. Weather, events, and people all have an impact on the ideal time to visit Ibiza.

The peak season in Ibiza lasts from June through September when the island is at its busiest. The island is overwhelmed with guests during this season, and hotel and activity prices are at their highest. The weather is often hot and dry, with average temperatures ranging from 26°C to 30°C. The island, on the other hand, may become quite hot throughout the day, and the beaches can get very crowded. If you're looking for a party atmosphere, now is the time to go. Ibiza is well-known for its vibrant nightlife, and the island comes alive during peak season with some of the world's greatest DJs performing at the island's many clubs.

If you want to take it easy, the best time to visit Ibiza is during the shoulder seasons. The shoulder seasons, which run from April to May and October to November, are great for avoiding crowds and enjoying a more relaxed holiday. Throughout these seasons, the weather remains nice, with temperatures ranging from 18°C to 24°C, making them excellent for outdoor activities. During specific seasons, costs for housing and activities are also decreased, and you may be able to take advantage of some excellent deals. However, since not all clubs and pubs are open throughout these seasons, the nightlife is not as active as it is during peak season.

Another factor to consider while choosing the best time to visit Ibiza is the events that take place on the island. Ibiza is home to some of the world's most prestigious music events, which may attract massive crowds. The most prominent festivals take place during the peak season, with events such as the Ibiza Rocks Festival and the International Music Summit drawing thousands of travelers. If you want to attend one of these festivals, peak season is the best time to do it. These activities, however, should be avoided if you wish to avoid crowds and have a more enjoyable Christmas.

The weather is an important factor to consider when determining when to visit Ibiza. The island's climate is Mediterranean, which means it has long, hot summers and mild winters. The peak season is the warmest time of year, with July and August being the hottest months. If you are susceptible to extreme heat, it is best to avoid visiting at this time. The shoulder seasons are an excellent choice, with temperatures that are warm enough for outdoor activities but not as scorching as the peak season.

The best time to visit Ibiza is influenced in part by the activities you choose to do. Summer is the best time to visit if you want to do water sports like jet skiing, paddle boarding, or snorkeling. The water is warm and calm, making it perfect for a variety of activities. The island also has some beautiful hiking trails that are best explored in the spring and autumn when the temperatures are cooler.

How to get to Ibiza

Traveling to Ibiza is straightforward, with several transportation options available based on your location and budget.

The most convenient way to go to Ibiza is via the airline. Ibiza has its airport, which is located around 7.5 kilometers southwest of Ibiza Town. Many airlines provide direct flights from major European cities such as London, Paris, and Amsterdam to Ibiza. You may use airline websites or travel aggregator websites like Expedia or Kayak to check flight availability and purchase tickets online.

If you're coming from inside Spain, you may take a domestic flight to Ibiza from Madrid or Barcelona. Domestic flights to Ibiza are offered by many airlines, including Iberia, Vueling, and Air Europa. Domestic flights are often less costly than international flights, making them an excellent choice if you're on a limited budget.

Ferries are another way to travel to Ibiza. Many ferry companies operate between the Spanish mainland and Ibiza, including Denia, Valencia, and Barcelona. The boat voyage takes between 3 and 8 hours depending on where you leave, and the price varies depending on the kind of seat or cabin you choose.

If you're coming from somewhere in Europe, you may take a ferry from ports in Italy, France, or Morocco. However, since these journeys may run up to 24 hours or longer, it's critical to plan ahead of time and reserve your tickets.

When traveling by boat to Ibiza, keep in mind that weather conditions may cause delays. Due to severe waves, ferry services to Ibiza may be reduced or canceled during the winter months, so check the schedules and weather conditions before purchasing your tickets.

It is also feasible to go to Ibiza by bus or automobile from the Spanish mainland. Bus connections to Ibiza are available from major Spanish towns like Madrid, Barcelona, and Valencia. The journey might take anywhere from 12 to 18 hours depending on the starting point, and prices vary depending on the kind of seat or cabin you choose.

You may take a ferry from Denia or Valencia to Ibiza and then hire a car on the island if you like. There are many car rental companies on the island, including Hertz, Avis, and Europcar, and prices vary depending on the kind of car and the rental length.

If you are traveling to Ibiza from outside of Europe, you may need to connect to a major European city before boarding a direct aircraft or ferry to Ibiza. British Airways, Air France, and Lufthansa are just a few of the major airlines that provide connections to Ibiza.

Packing Essentials

Whether you are planning to visit Ibiza for a long weekend or a week-long vacation, packing the right essentials is essential for a comfortable and enjoyable stay. In this guide, we will discuss the top packing essentials for an Ibiza visit.

- Sunscreen: Ibiza is renowned for its sunny weather, thus it is important to protect your skin from the sun's damaging rays. A high-SPF sunscreen is required for your trip to Ibiza. Pack enough sunscreen to last the duration of your vacation, and reapply it often throughout the day.
- Sunglasses: A pair of sunglasses, in addition to sunscreen, is a must-have for every trip to Ibiza. They not only shield your eyes from the brightness of the sun, but they also provide a fashionable touch to your attire. Pack a strong pair of sunglasses that can survive the island's bustling nightlife.
- Swimwear: Ibiza is the ideal place for swimming and sunbathing, thanks to its beautiful beaches and crystal-clear seas. Pack enough swimwear for your whole vacation, and choose materials that dry quickly and are pleasant to wear.
- Bag for the beach: A beach bag is crucial for transporting all of your beach supplies. Look for a bag that can accommodate your towel, sunscreen, sunglasses, and any other beach necessities. If you want to spend a lot of time in the water, invest in a waterproof bag.

- Comfortable Shoes: While Ibiza is famous for its partying, you should also see the island's natural beauty. Make sure you bring along a pair of good walking or trekking shoes. Sneakers or trekking boots are excellent choices.
- Casual Clothing: Ibiza is a laid-back vacation, so bring casual clothes that are both comfortable and breathable. Pack a variety of shorts, skirts, and dresses in lightweight materials such as cotton or linen.
- Party Outfits: Ibiza is famed for its nightlife, so bring some party clothes for your vacation. Look for clothing that is both fashionable and comfy, and don't be afraid to experiment with bright colors and patterns.
- Portable Charger: A portable charger is a must-have for any vacation to Ibiza, with all the images you'll be shooting and the necessity to remain connected. Pack a charger with enough juice to last the duration of your journey.
- Water Bottle: Staying hydrated is critical throughout your stay in Ibiza, particularly during the hot months. To combat dehydration, bring a reusable water bottle that you may refill during the day.
- Insect Repellent: While Ibiza is a lovely location, it is also a haven for mosquitoes and other biting insects. Pack bug repellant to prevent getting bitten, particularly if you want to spend time outside.
- Hat: A hat is an excellent complement to any trip to Ibiza since it provides extra sun protection. Look for a hat that is both fashionable and offers enough shade for your face and neck.
- Sweater or light jacket: While Ibiza is famed for its beautiful weather, the nights, particularly during the shoulder seasons, may be cold. To keep comfortable in the night, bring a light jacket or sweater.
- First Aid Kit:While no one likes to worry about being ill or wounded while on vacation in Ibiza, it is always preferable to be prepared. Pack a compact first-aid kit with essential medical items like bandages and pain medications.
- Travel Adapter: Because Ibiza utilizes European standard electrical outlets, you will need a travel converter to charge your electronic gadgets if you are visiting from a nation that uses a different standard electrical

outlet. Pack a travel adaptor that is compatible with the electrical outlets in Ibiza.

- Camera: Ibiza is a photographer's dream, with its magnificent natural beauty and bustling nightlife. Pack a camera to record all of your trip's great moments.

- Credit Cards and Cash: While many Ibiza shops take credit cards, it is usually a good idea to have extra cash on hand for little purchases and gratuities. Pack both cash and credit cards, and put them in a safe location.

- Passport or ID: If you are visiting Ibiza from a nation other than the European Union, you must have your passport with you. Even if you are coming from an EU nation, you need to have some sort of identification with you.

- Toiletries: Don't forget to bring your toothbrush, toothpaste, shampoo, conditioner, and soap with you. To comply with airport security restrictions, put these goods in a transparent plastic bag while traveling.

- Documents for Travel: Pack any additional trip papers you may need, such as your flight schedule or hotel bookings, in addition to your passport or ID.

- Snacks: While Ibiza has many restaurants and cafés, it is always a good idea to bring some snacks with you in case you become hungry in between meals. Bring some nutritious snacks with you, such as almonds, apples, or granola bars.

- Reusable Tote Bag: A reusable tote bag is an excellent eco-friendly alternative to plastic bags, and it may also be used to transport souvenirs or groceries.

- Earplugs: If you are a light sleeper or sensitive to noise, bring earplugs with you to help you get a good night's sleep, particularly if you will be staying in a crowded location.

- Travel Pillow: If you're taking a long flight or bus to Ibiza, a travel cushion may help make the trip more pleasant. Look for a travel cushion that is lightweight and small and simple to pack.

- Travel Insurance: when no one likes to consider mishaps or crises when traveling, it is always preferable to be prepared. Consider obtaining travel insurance to protect yourself in the event of an unforeseen occurrence, such as a flight cancellation or a medical emergency.

Chapter 2: Ibiza Accommodation and Cost

Ibiza is a well-known tourist destination that attracts people from all over the world. This wonderful Mediterranean island is well-known for its vibrant nightlife, pristine waters, and stunning beaches. Ibiza has plenty to offer everyone, whether you desire a luxurious holiday, a low-cost option, or everything in between.

In Ibiza, there are various options for accommodation. There are several alternatives to suit every taste and budget, ranging from luxurious villas to low-cost hostels. The kind of accommodation, the location, and the particular season of year all affect how much it costs to stay in Ibiza. This guide will look at the many types of homes in Ibiza and their associated prices.

Hotels

Ibiza has a wide range of hotels to suit all budgets, from cheap hotels to luxury resorts. The bulk of hotels are located in popular tourist areas like San Antonio, Playa d'en Bossa, and Ibiza Town. The price of a hotel room in Ibiza varies depending on the location and facilities offered. Budget hotels may range from €30 to €50 per night, while luxury resorts can cost up to €500 per night.

Apartments

Renting an apartment is a popular choice for many visitors to Ibiza, especially those staying for an extended period. Ibiza apartments vary in size and location, from little studios to massive, sumptuous penthouses. The majority of Ibiza apartments are fully furnished and equipped with modern amenities like air conditioning and Wi-Fi. Renting an apartment in Ibiza is priced differently depending on its location, size, and amenities. A small studio apartment may cost between €50 and €100 per night, whilst a stunning penthouse could cost between €500 and €600 per night.

Villas

Renting a villa is a popular choice for families and larger groups visiting Ibiza. The size and location of Ibiza villas vary from small, budget-friendly homes to massive, lavish villas with private pools and stunning sea views. The majority of Ibiza villas are fully furnished and equipped with modern amenities like air conditioning, Wi-Fi, and cable TV. The cost of renting a villa in Ibiza depends on its location, size, and amenities. A small, budget-friendly villa may cost between €100 and €200 per night, but a large, sumptuous villa can cost up to €2000 per night.

Hostels

Hostels are a popular choice for budget-conscious Ibiza tourists. The bulk of Ibiza hostels are located in popular tourist areas such as San Antonio, Playa d'en Bossa, and Ibiza Town. Ibiza hostels provide dormitory-style housing in which guests share a room with other vacationers. Certain hostels also provide private rooms with en-suite bathrooms. Hostels in Ibiza provide basic amenities such as Wi-Fi and a communal kitchen. The price of a hostel stay in Ibiza varies depending on location and room type. A bed in a dormitory-style room may cost €10 to €20 per night, whilst a private room may cost between €50 and €100 a night.

Camping

Camping is a popular choice for adventurous Ibiza tourists. There are several campsites on the island, most of them are located in rural areas away from the tourist crowds. Camping in Ibiza offers a one-of-a-kind experience, enabling visitors to admire the island's natural beauty while resting in a tent or caravan. The majority of Ibiza campsites include basic amenities such as toilets and showers. The cost of camping in Ibiza varies depending on the campsite and kind of accommodation. A tent costs €10-20 per night to pitch, whereas a caravan costs €50-100 per night to rent.

Airbnb

Airbnb is a popular lodging choice for many visitors to Ibiza. Airbnb offers a wide range of housing options, from cheap flats to luxury mansions. The bulk of Airbnb properties in Ibiza are located in popular tourist areas such as San Antonio, Playa d'en Bossa, and Ibiza Town. Airbnb flats in Ibiza are completely furnished and have modern amenities such as air conditioning, Wi-Fi, and cable TV. The cost of renting an Airbnb property in Ibiza depends on the location, size, and amenities. A low-cost hotel may cost €30-50 per night, whilst a luxurious villa may cost up to €1000 per night.

Where to stay in each city in Ibiza

When it comes to selecting the right spot to stay, the island offers a vast choice of alternatives to pick from, with options to fit all likes and budgets. In this guide, we'll look at some of the finest places to stay in each city in Ibiza, including prices and facilities for each kind of accommodation.

Ibiza Town

Ibiza Town, commonly known as Eivissa, is the island's capital and one of the most famous tourist sites. This vibrant city is known for its historic attractions, stylish shops, and restaurants. If you're searching for a place to stay in Ibiza Town, there are lots of possibilities.

- Budget: Hostels in Ibiza Town are an excellent choice for those on a tight budget. Prices usually vary between €15 and €30 per night. The majority of hostels include basic amenities including Wi-Fi, laundry facilities, and community kitchens.
- Mid-range: There are lots of mid-range hotels in Ibiza Town if you want a little more comfort and solitude. Prices per night vary from €50 to €150. Air conditioning, private toilets, and breakfast are among the services provided by these hotels.
- Luxury: There are various luxury hotels in Ibiza Town for people who wish to spend. Prices per night might vary from €300 to €1,000. These hotels provide features like infinity pools, spas, and ocean views.

San Antonio

San Antonio is a busy resort town on Ibiza's western coast. It is well-known for its magnificent beaches, vibrant nightlife, and breathtaking sunsets. San Antonio provides something for everyone, whether you want to party or rest.

- Budget: San Antonio has several hostels that appeal to budget-conscious guests. The nightly rate ranges from €15 to €30. These hostels include basic amenities including Wi-Fi, laundry services, and community kitchens.
- Mid-range: There are lots of mid-range hotels in San Antonio if you want a little more comfort and solitude. Prices per night vary from €50 to €150. Air conditioning, private toilets, and breakfast are among the services provided by these hotels.

- Luxury: There are numerous high-end hotels in San Antonio for customers seeking luxury. Prices per night might vary from €300 to €1,000. Private pools, wellness facilities, and ocean views are available at these hotels.

Santa Eulalia

Santa Eulalia is a lovely village on Ibiza's eastern coast. It is well-known for its lovely marina, charming shops, and beautiful beaches. Santa Eulalia is the ideal spot to stay if you want a more peaceful and serene environment.

- Budget: Santa Eulalia has a variety of low-cost lodging alternatives, including hostels and guesthouses. Prices per night vary from €20 to €50. These lodgings include basic facilities such as Wi-Fi and breakfast.
- Mid-range: There are various mid-range hotels in Santa Eulalia if you want more comfort and seclusion. Prices per night vary from €50 to €150. Air conditioning, private toilets, and breakfast are among the services provided by these hotels.
- Luxury: There are various luxury hotels in Santa Eulalia for people who wish to indulge. Prices per night might vary from €300 to €1,000. Private pools, wellness facilities, and ocean views are available at these hotels.

Playa d'en Bossa

Playa d'en Bossa is one of the island's most popular beach locations. It is noted for its vibrant atmosphere, crystal-clear seas, and fashionable beach clubs and is situated on Ibiza's southern coast.

- Budget: Budget-conscious visitors to Playa d'en Bossa might consider staying in hostels or guesthouses. Prices per night vary from €15 to €50. These lodgings include basic facilities such as Wi-Fi and breakfast.
- Mid-range: There are various mid-range hotels in Playa d'en Bossa if

you want a little more comfort and seclusion. Prices per night vary from €50 to €200. Air conditioning, private toilets, and breakfast are among the services provided by these hotels.

- Luxury: There are numerous high-end hotels in Playa d'en Bossa for guests seeking luxury. Prices per night might vary from €300 to €1,000. Private pools, wellness facilities, and ocean views are available at these hotels.

Cala Llonga

Cala Llonga is a tiny tourist town on Ibiza's eastern coast. It is well-known for its beautiful bay, laid-back environment, and family-friendly activities.

- Budget: Cala Llonga has a variety of low-cost lodging alternatives, including hostels and guesthouses. Prices per night vary from €20 to €50. These lodgings include basic facilities such as Wi-Fi and breakfast.
- Mid-range: There are various mid-range hotels in Cala Llonga if you want more comfort and seclusion. Prices per night vary from €50 to €150. Air conditioning, private toilets, and breakfast are among the services provided by these hotels.
- Luxury: There are various luxury hotels in Cala Llonga for people who wish to spend. Prices per night might vary from €300 to €1,000. Private pools, wellness facilities, and ocean views are available at these hotels.

Es Canar

Es Canar is a tiny tourist town on Ibiza's eastern coast. It's famous for its beautiful beach, relaxed ambiance, and monthly hippy market.

- Budget: Es Canar has a variety of low-cost accommodations, including hostels and guesthouses. Prices per night vary from €20 to €50. These lodgings include basic facilities such as Wi-Fi and breakfast.
- Mid-range: There are various mid-range hotels in Es Canar if you want

more comfort and seclusion. Prices per night vary from €50 to €150. Air conditioning, private toilets, and breakfast are among the services provided by these hotels.

- Luxury: There are numerous high-end hotels in Es Canar for customers seeking luxury. Prices per night might vary from €300 to €1,000. Private pools, wellness facilities, and ocean views are available at these hotels.

Chapter 3: Visa and Entry Requirements

I f you want to visit Ibiza as a tourist, you should be aware of the visa and entrance requirements before making your travel plans.

Ibiza Visa Requirements

Ibiza is a Spanish island that is a member of the European Union. If you are a citizen of an EU nation, such as Switzerland, Norway, Iceland, or Liechtenstein, you do not require a visa to visit Spain, including Ibiza. Without a visa, you may remain in the nation for up to 90 days in six months.

You may require a visa to enter Spain if you are not a citizen of one of these countries. The kind of visa you need is determined by the purpose and duration of your travel. For example, if you want to visit Ibiza for tourist reasons for fewer than 90 days, a Schengen visa may be required.

Ibiza Schengen Visa

The Schengen visa is a kind of visa that permits non-EU nationals to visit Spain and other Schengen nations for tourism, business, or other reasons for up to 90 days in six months. The Spanish embassy or consulate in your country of residence issues the Schengen visa.

You have to provide the following papers to get a Schengen visa for Ibiza:

- A current passport
- A fully filled-out visa application
- Two passport photographs
- Proof of trip arrangements (flight tickets, hotel reservations, and so on).
- Financial evidence (bank statements, credit card statements, etc.)
- Travel medical insurance
- Proof of links to your home country (job letter, ownership of property, etc.)

The cost of a Schengen visa for Ibiza varies based on your home country. As of 2023, the regular Schengen visa price is €80 for adults and €40 for minors aged 6 to 12. The visa cost is waived for children under the age of six.

Other Visa Options for Ibiza

If you want to visit Ibiza for another reason, such as a job, study, or a long-term stay, you may need a different sort of visa. If you want to work in Ibiza, you'll need a work visa, and if you want to study there, you'll need a student visa.

These visa requirements vary based on the kind of visa and the duration of your stay. For further information on the exact criteria and processes for these kinds of visas, contact the Spanish embassy or consulate in your place of residence.

Ibiza Entry Requirements

In addition to visa requirements, you must also fulfill entrance criteria to visit Ibiza as a tourist. These are some examples:

- A current passport: You must have a valid passport that is valid for at least six months after your arrival date in Ibiza.
- Return flight: You must have a return ticket or evidence of further travel,

such as a reservation for another airline, bus, or train.

- Sufficient funds: You must have enough money to cover your stay in Ibiza, including lodging, food, and other expenditures. The amount of money needed depends on the duration and purpose of your visit.
- Travel medical insurance: You must have travel health insurance that covers medical bills and repatriation if you get sick or injured while in Ibiza. The insurance must cover emergency medical care, hospitalization, and repatriation for the length of your stay.
- COVID-19 specifications: Because of the COVID-19 pandemic, extra restrictions for entering Ibiza may exist, such as confirmation of vaccination, a negative COVID-19 test result, or quarantine upon arrival. These criteria may differ based on your place of origin and Ibiza's current COVID-19 condition. Before you go, be sure you have the most up-to-date information and requirements.

You should have no trouble visiting Ibiza as a tourist if you satisfy these prerequisites. It is crucial to understand, however, that border authorities have the authority to prohibit entrance if they feel you do not satisfy the entry criteria or constitute a danger to public health or security.

Travel Restrictions

Tourists visiting the Spanish island of Ibiza will be subject to a variety of travel restrictions beginning in 2023 to safeguard public safety and limit the spread of the COVID-19 virus. These limits have been implemented to aid in the containment of the current epidemic, which has caused major disruption to the global travel economy.

To begin, all visitors to Ibiza will be forced to provide proof of a negative COVID-19 test result before entering the island. This requirement will apply to all travelers, regardless of whether or not they have been inoculated against the virus. The test must be completed within 72 hours after arrival, and the findings must be submitted to authorities.

In addition to testing, visitors to Ibiza will be required to complete a health declaration form before arrival. This questionnaire will elicit information about the traveler's recent travel history, potential COVID-19 exposure, and any symptoms they may be experiencing. The purpose of this form is to aid authorities in detecting potential COVID-19 infections and isolating and treating infected people.

Another restraint that visitors to Ibiza will face is the need to follow social distancing procedures. Wearing face masks in public areas, maintaining at least two meters away from other people, and avoiding large gatherings or groups will be among the measures. Failure to follow these processes may result in penalties or other repercussions.

Temperature testing will also be performed on visitors to Ibiza upon arrival and at other times during their stay. If a tourist is diagnosed with COVID-19 fever or other symptoms, they may be required to undergo further testing or quarantine to prevent the virus from spreading.

Furthermore, specific locations or attractions on the island may have additional restrictions or requirements. Some well-known nightclubs and other entertainment venues, for example, may have capacity restrictions or require proof of immunization or a negative COVID-19 test result before entrance.

Tourists visiting Ibiza should be aware of these boundaries and respect all laws and regulations to ensure their safety as well as the safety of the local population. Failure to adhere to these guidelines may result in fines or other penalties, as well as contribute to the spread of the virus and major delays in travel and tourism.

While some passengers may find these restrictions inconvenient, they are necessary to aid in the management of the present outbreak and the preservation of public health. Further limitations or procedures may be imposed in the future as the situation unfolds, and passengers should be prepared to react to any changes that arise.

Consider Ibiza travel insurance.

Ibiza is a well-known tourist destination known for its frenetic nightlife, beautiful beaches, and rich cultural past. If you are planning a trip to Ibiza, you should consider purchasing travel insurance to protect yourself against any unforeseen events that may occur during your trip.

Ibiza travel insurance often covers medical expenses, trip cancellation or interruption, lost or stolen luggage, and emergency evacuation. Medical coverage is particularly important since medical treatment in Ibiza may be expensive for tourists who are not covered by the Spanish national health system.

When getting Ibiza travel insurance, it is essential to consider the quantity of coverage you need. If you wish to participate in adventure sports or other high-risk activities, for example, you may require more comprehensive insurance that covers injuries sustained as a consequence of such activities.

Other important aspects to consider while choosing Ibiza travel insurance are the policy's limitations and limits. Some policies may not cover pre-existing medical conditions or certain types of injuries, so it is crucial to read the policy completely and understand what is and is not covered.

When choosing Ibiza travel insurance, you should also consider the length of your trip. Many policies have a maximum trip duration of 30 or 60 days, so if you want to stay in Ibiza for an extended period, you may need to purchase several policies or find a policy with a longer maximum trip length.

When searching for Ibiza travel insurance, compare policies from many providers to get the best coverage at the best price. Using online comparison tools, you may compare plans from numerous providers and get costs based on your specific needs.

Some Ibiza travel insurance policies may also include add-ons like 24-hour emergency support, transportation aid, and concierge services. These benefits are especially valuable if you are visiting Ibiza for the first time and are unfamiliar with the local language and customs.

It is essential to properly study the policy documents and comprehend the coverage's terms and restrictions before purchasing Ibiza travel insurance. Check with your credit card company or other insurance providers to determine whether your coverage overlaps with the Ibiza travel insurance policy.

Aside from purchasing Ibiza travel insurance, you may take further steps to safeguard yourself while on holiday in Ibiza. Here are a few examples:

- Keeping a copy of your passport and other important documents in a safe place, such as a hotel safe or an online storage service.
- Being aware of your surroundings and avoiding potentially hazardous or unexpected environments.
- Staying hydrated and avoiding excessive alcohol consumption is especially crucial if you want to participate in high-risk activities.
- To secure your belongings, take basic precautions such as locking your hotel room door and wearing a money belt.

Helpful Ibiza apps to download

If you're planning a trip to Ibiza, there are a few apps that may help make your stay more enjoyable and stress-free. These apps can help you make the most of your trip to Ibiza, from finding the best places to eat and drink to getting about the island.

The Ibiza Bus app is one of the most useful for visitors to Ibiza. This app provides real-time information on the bus schedules, routes, and fares on the island. By utilizing the Ibiza Bus app, you can plan your excursions ahead of time, avoid long lineups at bus stops, and save money on transportation.

Another must-have for vacationers is the Ibiza Beaches app. This app provides detailed information on the island's beaches, such as their location, amenities, and water quality. The Ibiza Beaches app can help you choose the best beach for your needs, whether you desire a secluded cove or a crowded party atmosphere.

If you want to learn more about Ibiza's nightlife culture, the Ibiza Clubbing app is an excellent resource. This app provides information on all of the island's clubs, including their location, music genre, and upcoming events. With the Ibiza Clubbing app, you can plan your nights out in advance, avoid long lines at the door, and discover new clubs and DJs.

The Eat Ibiza app is a wonderful resource for anyone interested in learning more about Ibiza's culinary culture. This app provides information about the island's best restaurants, cafés, and bars, as well as user reviews and ratings. With the Eat Ibiza app, you can discover new culinary experiences, avoid tourist traps, and find the best places to eat and drink in Ibiza.

Ibiza Maps is another useful tool for visitors. This application offers street maps, hiking trails, public transportation routes, and island-wide maps. With the Ibiza Maps app, you can easily traverse the island, discover its hidden corners, and find the best spots for hiking, cycling, and other outdoor sports.

If you're heading to Ibiza with a group of friends, the Splitwise app may help you split expenses and avoid disputes. This tool enables you to manage shared expenditures, distribute invoices, and pay debts in a timely and easy manner. Using the Splitwise app, you can keep track of your spending, avoid misunderstandings, and enjoy your holiday without worrying about money.

The Ibiza History app is a great way to learn about Ibiza's history and culture. This app recounts the island's rich history, which includes ancient civilizations, medieval fortresses, and cultural riches. With the Ibiza Past app, you can discover the island's hidden beauties, learn about its unique past, and appreciate its distinct cultural heritage.

Finally, anybody planning a trip to Ibiza should download the Ibiza Weather app. This app displays current Ibiza weather conditions such as temperature, humidity, wind speed, and precipitation. The Ibiza Weather app can help you plan your outside activities, carry proper gear, and avoid unpleasant shocks caused by weather changes.

Ibiza Emergency Contacts

Ibiza is a well-known tourist destination noted for its lively nightlife and beautiful beaches. As a guest, you should be aware of the emergency contacts available on the island in case of any difficulties that arise during your stay. Here are the emergency phone numbers to keep in mind while visiting Ibiza.

The first and most important contact to know in Ibiza is the emergency number. In an emergency, whether it's a medical emergency or a police situation, phone 112. This number is available 24 hours a day, seven days a week, and may be reached from any phone, including mobile phones.

In the event of an emergency, it is important to have the contact information for Ibiza's hospitals and clinics on hand. The major hospital on the island is Can Misses Hospital in Ibiza Town. It has a 24-hour emergency department and offers a wide range of medical services. On the island, several private clinics provide medical services, such as Policlinica Nuestra Seora del Rosario in Ibiza Town and Clinica Picasso in San Antonio.

062 is the number to dial if you need to contact the police. This number is available 24 hours a day, seven days a week, and may be reached by phone.

The police station in Ibiza Town may be reached at +34 971 19 90 00, while the police station in San Antonio can be reached at +34 971 34 00 47.

085 is the number to phone in the case of a fire. This number is available 24 hours a day, seven days a week, and may be reached by phone. The fire department in Ibiza may be reached at +34 971 31 21 15.

Contact your local embassy or consulate if you need to report a lost or stolen passport. The British Consulate in Ibiza may be reached at +34 93 366 6200, while the US Consulate in Barcelona can be reached at +34 93 280 2227.

If a natural disaster or severe weather occurs, you should monitor local news channels or visit the Balearic Islands Government's website for information and recommendations.

Aside from these emergency contacts, it's a good idea to be aware of other useful connections while in Ibiza. Call Radio Taxi Ibiza at +34 971 39 84 83 or +34 971 39 37 83 if you need a taxi. For general information about the island, contact the Ibiza Tourist Office at +34 971 30 19 00 or visit their website.

What vaccinations do I need?

As a traveler to Ibiza, you must have all of the necessary vaccinations. While Ibiza is generally a safe destination to visit, certain health risks come with visiting any foreign country, and being vaccinated is an important way to protect yourself.

The vaccines you need will depend on your age, health, and any pre-existing medical conditions. There are, however, a few vaccines that all visitors to Ibiza must-have.

To begin, ensure that you have had all of your routine vaccinations, including measles, mumps, and rubella (MMR), diphtheria, tetanus, pertussis (DTaP), and varicella (chickenpox). These vaccines, which are often taken during childhood, are recommended for all travelers, regardless of destination.

In addition to routine vaccinations, a few extra vaccines may be recommended for your trip to Ibiza. One such inoculation that is advised for all tourists to Spain is the hepatitis A vaccination. Hepatitis A is caused by a viral virus that is transferred by contaminated food or water, and vaccination is a great way to protect yourself from this illness.

Another vaccine that may be recommended for an Ibiza vacation is the hepatitis B vaccination. Hepatitis B is a viral infection that can be transmitted through blood or other bodily fluids, and the vaccine is recommended for travelers who may be at higher risk of exposure, such as those who plan to have sexual contact with locals or seek medical treatment while in Ibiza.

If you want to spend a significant amount of time outdoors in Ibiza, you should consider being vaccinated against tick-borne encephalitis (TBE). TBE is a viral infection carried by infected tick bites that are especially common in rural areas of Europe. While the risk of TBE is low in Ibiza, it is something to consider if you plan to spend a lot of time hiking or camping.

Another vaccine that may be recommended for Ibiza tourists is meningococcal immunization. Meningococcal infection is a bacterial infection that may cause meningitis. It is spread by close contact with an infected individual or contact with contaminated droplets. Travelers who plan to stay in hostels or other communal accommodations, or who plan to attend large gatherings or festivals, may be more susceptible to meningococcal disease and may benefit from this immunization.

Visitors to Ibiza may also benefit from a rabies vaccine, particularly if they plan to engage in outdoor activities or interact with animals such as bats or stray dogs. Rabies is a viral virus that produces severe neurological symptoms and is spread via the saliva of infected animals.

Aside from these vaccinations, there are a few more precautions you should take before visiting Ibiza. Keep your hands clean, for example, and avoid contact with animals, since both may be causes of infection. You should also take steps to prevent mosquito bites, since mosquitos in Ibiza may transmit a variety of ailments, including dengue fever and the Zika virus.

Download the offline map

Having access to maps as a tourist to Ibiza is essential for exploring the island's different attractions. However, many visitors may not have internet access or may prefer not to use data while seeing the island. In such cases, downloading Ibiza's offline map is your best bet.

Downloading the offline map of Ibiza is a simple process that may be completed via several methods. The first step is to choose an offline mapping tool to use. The most popular offline map applications are Maps.me, Google Maps, and CityMaps2Go.

Install the Maps.me app on your smartphone or tablet first to receive an offline map of Ibiza. Launch the app after installing it and put "Ibiza" into the search area. The software will then display a map of Ibiza, which you can zoom in and out to explore the areas you choose to visit.

Then you must get an offline map of Ibiza. Go to the bottom of the screen and click the "Download" button to do so. The application will then prompt you to choose a place for the download. After you've decided on a place, click the "Download" button once again, and the map will begin to download. The download time will vary depending on the size of the map and the speed of your internet connection.

If you prefer to utilize Google Maps, open it and search for "Ibiza." When the

Ibiza map is shown, click on the three horizontal lines in the top left corner of the screen. This will bring up a menu from which you may choose "Offline maps." Then, choose "Select your map" and the application will allow you to select the area to download. After selecting a place, click the "Download" button to begin downloading the map.

Finally, you may download an offline map of Ibiza using the CityMaps2Go app. To do so, open the app and type in "Ibiza." The application will display an Ibiza map, which you can download by pressing the "Download" button at the bottom of the screen. This will prompt you to choose the area from which to download. After you've decided on a place, click the "Download" button once again, and the map will begin to download.

For visitors to the island, downloading an offline map of Ibiza is an excellent idea. It allows you to navigate the island without needing to use data or connect to the internet. It may also be handy while visiting places with little or no internet connectivity, such as remote beaches or towns.

One advantage of downloading an offline map is that you may be able to save battery life. When utilizing an online map, your device's GPS receiver must be always active, which quickly drains your battery. However, with an offline map, you may turn off your device's data connection and still use the map.

Another benefit of downloading an offline map is that you may plan your travels. You may use an offline map to mark the locations you want to visit and find the most efficient route to get there. This helps you to make the most of your vacation to Ibiza by maximizing your time.

Additionally, an offline map may be quite handy for those who do not know Spanish fluently, since it allows you to navigate the island without having to talk with locals. The offline map will display street names and destinations in English, making it easier for tourists to understand and follow directions. This is particularly useful when traveling to remote places with fewer English-speaking residents.

It is also worth noting that using an offline map may be safer than using an online map. When you use an online map, you may be revealing your location and data to third-party organizations, putting your privacy at risk. With an offline map, you don't have to worry about such concerns since your location data is only stored on your smartphone.

Learn basic phrases

It is usually beneficial for a visitor visiting Ibiza to acquire some fundamental words in the native language, which is Spanish. This will allow you to converse with the people and enjoy your stay more. We will give you a list of fundamental words to learn before visiting Ibiza in this guide.

- Hola – This is the most basic Spanish greeting, meaning "hello." It is used to introduce yourself to someone for the first time. It may also be used to express good-bye.
- Adiós – This is the Spanish term for saying "goodbye." It is appropriate to utilize it while leaving a location or saying goodbye to someone.
- Por favor – This phrase means "please" and is used when requesting or asking for something.
- Gracias – This is the Spanish equivalent of "thank you." You may use it to convey your appreciation for what someone has done for you.
- De nada – This phrase translates to "you're welcome" and is used in response to someone thanking you.
- ¿Cómo estás? – This is a frequent phrase in Spanish that means "How are you?" You may use it to strike up a discussion or to inquire how someone is feeling.
- Estoy perdido – This phrase means "I'm lost" and can help you find your way around Ibiza.
- ¿Dónde está…? – This phrase means "where is…" and is used to request directions to a particular location, such as a hotel, beach, or restaurant.

- No hablo español – This phrase means "I don't speak Spanish" and may help you communicate with someone who doesn't speak your language.
- ¿Hablas inglés? – This phrase translates to "Do you speak English?" This is an effective approach to asking someone whether they speak English.
- Lo siento – This phrase means "I'm sorry" and may be used to express regret for anything you've done wrong.
- Buenos días – This is a greeting in Spanish that means "good morning." You may use it in the morning to welcome someone.
- Buenas tardes – This is a greeting in Spanish that means "good afternoon." In the afternoon, you may use it to welcome someone.
- Buenas noches – This is a greeting in Spanish that means "good evening" or "good night." It is appropriate to use it to welcome someone in the evening or before going to bed.
- Una cerveza, por favor – This phrase means "a beer, please" and is handy when ordering a beverage at a bar or restaurant.
- Una botella de agua, por favor – This phrase means "a bottle of water, please" and is handy when ordering water at a bar or restaurant.
- La cuenta, por favor – This phrase means "the bill, please" and is handy when asking for the bill in a restaurant.
- ¿Cuánto cuesta? – This phrase means "How much does it cost?" and can be useful when you are shopping or buying something.
- No entiendo – This phrase translates to "I don't understand" and may be used when you don't understand what someone is saying.
- Me gustaría reservar una mesa – This phrase indicates "I would like to reserve a table" and is handy when making a restaurant reservation.
- ¿Dónde puedo comprar…? – This phrase means "Where can I buy…" and may be used to inquire about the availability of a certain item or product.
- ¿Cómo llego a…? – This phrase implies "how do I get to…" and might be handy when looking for directions to a certain location.
- Está bien – This phrase means "it's okay" or "alright" and may be used to express agreement or to convey that everything is OK.
- Lo siento, no puedo – This phrase means "I'm sorry, but I can't" and is used to decline an invitation or request.

- ¡Buen provecho! – This phrase means "Enjoy your meal!" and is a polite way of saying "Good meal!"
- Me gusta/I dislike - These expressions, which mean "I like" and "I don't like," may be used to communicate your preferences.
- Quiero ir a la playa – This phrase means "I want to go to the beach" and may be used to express your desire to visit the beach.

Familiarize yourself with the currency

As a visitor to Ibiza, you should get acquainted with the island's money. The euro (€) is the currency of Ibiza, and it is also used across Spain. This implies that if you've visited other regions of Spain before visiting Ibiza, you should be acquainted with the euro and how it operates.

Before going to Ibiza, it is suggested that you transfer your currency into euros since this generally results in better exchange rates than changing money at an Ibiza currency exchange station. Many banks and exchange offices provide currency exchange services, and it is important to compare conversion rates to get the best bargain.

Keep in mind that big amounts, such as €100 or €200 banknotes, may be declined while spending money in Ibiza. Carry smaller denominations of currency, such as €10 or €20 notes, to enable fast and easy transactions.

Credit cards are widely accepted in Ibiza, particularly at bigger facilities like hotels, restaurants, and stores. Having additional cash on hand, on the other hand, is typically a good idea in case you come across a small shop that does not take card payments. Furthermore, many restaurants may impose a fee for credit card transactions, so check beforehand.

It is also worth noting that, although some businesses take other currencies, such as the US dollar or the British pound, the exchange rate utilized may be unfavorable, resulting in a greater cost for your purchases. As a result, doing business in Ibiza using Euros is always preferred.

When exchanging currencies or making purchases in Ibiza, it is essential to be wary of any scams or fraudulent behavior. Exchange money only at recognized banks or exchange offices, and always double-check your change after each transaction. Also, be wary of anybody who offers to swap money on the street, since this might be a fraud.

ATMs are extensively distributed across Ibiza and provide a handy option to withdraw cash using a debit or credit card. However, it is critical to verify with your bank about any possible fees or limitations while using your card abroad. To prevent any possible issues, always utilize ATMs situated in safe and well-lit places.

You'll also need cash to tip, which is customary in Ibiza. Tipping in Ibiza is generally 10%, however, it is totally up to you. If you get outstanding service, feel free to tip extra. Keep in mind that certain restaurants may charge a service fee, so check before leaving a tip.

Ibiza may be an expensive resort in terms of costs, particularly during high season. The cost of food, beverages, and lodging may vary greatly depending on where you travel and when you go. Prices, for example, are often higher during the summer, when the island is at its busiest. Consider visiting Ibiza during the off-season, when rates are cheaper.

Health and safety considerations

Ibiza is a stunning Mediterranean Sea island that is a popular tourist destination for travelers from all over the world. Tourists visiting Ibiza must take basic health and safety measures to guarantee a happy and safe stay.

Protecting oneself from the sun's harmful rays is one of the most critical health measures for tourists to Ibiza. The Mediterranean climate may be hot, and the sun's rays can cause sunburn and other skin problems. Wearing sunscreen, a hat, and other protective clothing is critical, especially during the hot summer months. To stay hydrated in the heat, tourists should drink plenty of water.

Another important health risk for visitors to Ibiza is food hygiene. Ibiza boasts a broad selection of restaurants and food vendors, but it is essential to choose properly. Tourists should only eat at reputable businesses, preferably those with high sanitation standards. Tourists should also avoid drinking tap water in favor of bottled water or other packaged beverages.

Travelers must be cautious while driving on Ibiza's roads in terms of safety. Roads may be narrow and twisty, and numerous vehicles may disobey traffic restrictions. Before you begin your journey, it is essential to rent a car from a reputable car rental company and verify the vehicle's condition. Tourists should also wear seat belts and follow speed limits.

Tourists should also be cautious of minor crimes such as pickpocketing and theft. Ibiza is well-known for its nightlife, and some may take advantage of the crowds to steal from travelers. To avoid such incidents, tourists must remain aware of their surroundings, keep valuables safe, and avoid carrying too much cash.

Aside from the aforementioned concerns, travelers must also be mindful of their alcohol consumption. Ibiza is known for its vibrant nightlife, and tourists may overindulge, leading to dangerous situations. Drink responsibly, don't accept drinks from strangers, and never drink and drive.

Another safety worry for travelers to Ibiza is the risk of drowning. Ibiza is surrounded by water, which may tempt people to swim in it. It is, however, vital to swim only in designated areas with lifeguards and other safety safeguards in place. Tourists should also avoid swimming alone and should never swim when under the influence of alcohol.

Tourists should be aware of the local norms and customs while visiting Ibiza. It is essential to respect local culture and traditions, especially while visiting sacred sites. Tourists should also dress modestly while visiting such places and avoid partaking in any behavior that may annoy the locals.

Finally, visitors to Ibiza should be prepared for medical emergencies. It is essential to have travel insurance that covers medical emergencies, accidents, and repatriation. Tourists should also include a basic first-aid kit that includes basic drugs and bandages.

Chapter 4: Understanding Ibiza Transaction Fees

As a tourist to Ibiza, you should be aware of the many transaction fees that you may encounter throughout your stay. Transaction fees are fees that you may be charged for each financial transaction you do, such as withdrawing money from an ATM or making a credit card purchase.

The ATM fee is one of the most common transaction expenses on the island of Ibiza. When you withdraw cash from an ATM, you will normally be charged a fee by both the ATM operator and your bank. These fees may vary depending on the bank and the ATM operator, so contact your bank before coming to Ibiza to find out how much you may be charged.

Another thing to consider while visiting Ibiza is the international transaction fee. Your bank will charge you this fee if you use your credit or debit card to conduct a foreign currency transaction. If you make any purchases while on vacation in Ibiza, foreign transaction fees, which may be a percentage of the total purchase amount or a flat cost, may quickly add up.

If you use your credit or debit card to withdraw cash from an ATM, you may be charged fees in addition to these transaction expenses. These are referred to as cash advance fees, and they may be levied by both your bank and the ATM operator. Cash advance fees, like foreign transaction fees, may quickly add up if you withdraw cash often with your credit or debit card.

To avoid these costs, bring a mix of cash and credit cards with you when you visit Ibiza. Cash is almost generally accepted on the island, and many businesses prefer cash over credit cards since it is faster to process and has no transaction fees. Credit cards, on the other hand, may be useful for larger purchases or signature-required transactions, such as renting a car or booking a hotel room.

Another option for reducing transaction expenses when visiting Ibiza is to use a prepaid travel card. These cards may be pre-loaded with cash and used similarly to a credit or debit card to make purchases or withdraw cash from ATMs. Prepaid travel cards may offer lower transaction fees than normal credit or debit cards, making them an excellent alternative for travelers wishing to avoid unexpected charges.

It's also important to be aware of any fees that your hotel or resort may levy during your stay in Ibiza. Some hotels and resorts impose resort fees or other additional expenses that are not included in the room rate. These rates may change depending on the location and the time of year, so check with your hotel before you arrive to learn about any fees that may apply during your stay.

Avoid cell phone roaming charges

One thing you should consider as an Ibiza tourist is how to avoid mobile phone roaming charges. Your mobile phone carrier will charge you roaming fees if you use your phone outside of your home network. These fees may be rather hefty, and they can quickly add up, especially if you use your phone often.

The good news is that there are many alternatives for avoiding roaming charges while visiting Ibiza. One of the most effective approaches is to buy a local SIM card. A SIM card is a little chip that, when inserted into your phone, enables you to connect to a local network. By obtaining a local SIM card, you will be able to use your phone normally without incurring any additional costs.

A local SIM card may be purchased in Ibiza from any mobile phone store or kiosk. These stores provide SIM cards designed specifically for travelers, with a variety of plans to choose from. Some plans provide unlimited data, while others offer a limited quantity of data, minutes, and messages. The cost of these plans varies according to the supplier and the plan chosen.

Another technique for reducing mobile phone roaming expenses while visiting Ibiza is to use a Wi-Fi hotspot. A Wi-Fi hotspot is a device that uses Wi-Fi to connect to the internet. Wi-Fi hotspots are available in the majority of Ibiza's cafés, hotels, and public venues. While connected to a Wi-Fi hotspot, you may use your phone to make calls and send messages without paying any additional expenses.

If you don't want to get a local SIM card or use a Wi-Fi hotspot, you may instead use messaging software. WhatsApp, Viber, and Skype are messaging apps that allow you to send and receive messages as well as make phone calls via the Internet. These apps are free to use and may be used from anywhere in the world with an internet connection. If you use a messaging app, you will be able to interact with your friends and relatives back home without incurring any additional expenses.

Another way to save money on mobile phone roaming is to turn off data roaming on your phone. Data roaming is a feature that allows you to use data when not connected to your home network. If you use data roaming, though, your mobile phone operator will charge you extra. To avoid these charges, turn off data roaming in your phone's settings.

You may also deactivate automatic app updates and background data in addition to data roaming. These features allow your apps to update and use data even when you are not actively using them. By turning off these services, you may save data and avoid unnecessary fees.

Finally, before visiting Ibiza, check with your cell phone provider to see whether they offer international plans or discounts. Some carriers provide special plans for international travelers that include lower rates for calls, texts, and data. Using these alternatives may help you save money and avoid unnecessary expenses.

Consider an Ibiza SIM card or Mifi device

As a tourist to Ibiza, having reliable and reasonably priced mobile data may significantly enhance your time on the island. One option is to get an Ibiza SIM card or Mifi device. In this piece, we'll look at the benefits of using a local SIM card or Mifi device in Ibiza, as well as some tips for making the most of your mobile data while on the island.

Let's start by defining a SIM card and a Mifi device. A SIM card is a little chip that may be inserted into a phone or other mobile device to offer cellular connectivity. In Ibiza, many mobile network companies offer prepaid SIM cards with varied data plans. In contrast, a Mifi device is a portable wireless hotspot that can connect to the internet through cellular networks and provide internet access to several devices at the same time. With a Mifi device, you may enjoy the convenience of having your own personal Wi-Fi network anywhere you go in Ibiza.

One of the key advantages of using a local SIM card or Mifi device in Ibiza is the potential to save money. While roaming expenses with a foreign SIM card may quickly add up, acquiring a local SIM card or Mifi device might provide a more cost-effective option for staying connected while in Ibiza. With a prepaid SIM card, you can easily limit your internet use and avoid unexpected charges. Furthermore, prepaid SIM cards in Ibiza often provide large data limits at cheap costs, making it easy to stay connected without breaking the bank.

Another benefit of using a local SIM card or Mifi device in Ibiza is improved connectivity. While there is public Wi-Fi in certain areas of the island, it may be intermittent and slow. With a local SIM card or Mifi device, you can enjoy a fast and consistent internet connection everywhere you go in Ibiza. This is particularly important if you want to use your smartphone for navigation, communication, or video streaming.

Furthermore, having mobile data access may make your Ibiza holiday more enjoyable and convenient. Using a local SIM card or Mifi device, you can easily stay in touch with friends and family back home, post updates on social media, and explore local sites and activities. Mobile data may also be used to make restaurant reservations, acquire club and event tickets, and request transportation services. With mobile data at your disposal, you can make the most of your time in Ibiza and move with ease.

When purchasing a local SIM card or Mifi device in Ibiza, it is essential to compare the coverage and data plans offered by different mobile network providers. While some providers may offer reduced rates, others may not provide complete coverage. Furthermore, before purchasing a SIM card, ensure that your mobile device is unlocked and compatible with the local network.

To get the most out of your mobile data in Ibiza, you may do several things after purchasing a local SIM card or Mifi device. To begin, you may download offline maps and travel directions to your mobile device before arriving in Ibiza. This will enable you to tour the island without exhausting your mobile data plan. Second, you can conserve data on your mobile device by eliminating automatic updates and background apps. Third, where available, utilize Wi-Fi hotspots to reduce your mobile data use.

Consider the adapter and converter

Ibiza is a well-known tourist resort in the Balearic Islands of Spain. One of the most important things to consider as a tourist to Ibiza is the kind of adapter and converter you will need for your electrical devices. This is because Ibiza, like the rest of Europe, has a different kind of electrical system than North America and the rest of the world.

The first difference to establish is between a converter and an adapter. An adapter is a little gadget that enables you to connect your electronic equipment to an unfamiliar country's electrical outlets. It does not change the voltage or frequency of the electrical current; rather, it adapts the plug to fit the outlet. A converter, on the other hand, is a larger device that alters the voltage and frequency of the electrical current to match the voltage and frequency of your device.

Ibiza's electrical outlets use a Type F plug, which has two circular prongs and a grounding pin. This kind of plug is also used in other European countries, such as Germany, Austria, and the Netherlands. You'll need an adapter if you're coming from North America to connect your Type A or Type B plug into a Type F outlet.

An adapter enables you to plug in your electronic devices, but it does not change the voltage or frequency of the electrical current. The electrical system in Ibiza operates at 230 volts and 50 hertz, as opposed to the 120 volts and 60 hertz used in North America. This means that if you connect equipment that isn't designed for 230 volts, it might be damaged or catch fire.

To avoid this, you will need to use a converter in addition to an adapter. A converter will alter the voltage and frequency of the electrical current to match the voltage and frequency of your equipment, ensuring safe and efficient operation. However, not all electrical equipment is compatible with converters, so double-check the voltage and frequency requirements of your gadgets before flying to Ibiza.

In addition to the Type F plug, certain Ibiza hotels and accommodations may include Type C outlets, which are also used in other European countries. These outlets have two circular pins but no grounding pin. If you come across this kind of outlet, you will need a Style C converter to fit your Kind A or Type B plug.

It should also be noted that Ibiza has a different electrical system than the rest of Spain. The island of Ibiza employs a Type F plug, whereas the rest of Spain uses a Type C plug. This implies that if you visit Ibiza and then go to another part of Spain, you may need a different kind of converter to plug in your electronic devices.

There are several options for purchasing adapters and converters. You may purchase them online before flying or at electronics or travel stores once you get to Ibiza. It is vital, however, that you get high-quality, trustworthy goods that are compatible with your contemporary devices.

Etiquette and customs

If you are planning a trip to Ibiza, you should be aware of the local customs and etiquette to have a pleasant and respectful stay.

Dressing appropriately is one of the most important traditions in Ibiza, especially while visiting religious sites. Women should cover their shoulders and dress in long skirts or trousers, while men should dress in long pants and sleeved shirts. It is also important to dress modestly while visiting local marketplaces and businesses.

Even if you don't know the person well, it's customary to welcome them with a cheek kiss. This is common in Spain and is meant to communicate respect and friendliness. It is important to note, however, that not everyone will be comfortable with this, so always ask before commencing the welcome.

It's also critical to respect Ibiza's natural siesta culture. Many shops and businesses close from 2 to 5 p.m., and people take time away from their usual jobs to rest and recharge. It is best to avoid making loud noises or engaging in activities that may disturb the peace at this time.

Environmental awareness is another important aspect of Ibiza's culture. The island is well-known for its natural beauty, and both inhabitants and tourists are expected to keep it clean and safeguard its natural resources. It is essential to properly dispose of trash to protect the sensitive ecosystems that make Ibiza so distinctive.

When it comes to dining etiquette, keep in mind that meals in Ibiza are often shared with family and friends. It is customary to share meals and take your time eating. A little tip, usually 5-10% of the total price, is also customary.

If you plan on attending one of Ibiza's famed nightlife events, there are a few things you should keep in mind. To begin, it is essential to follow the venue's dress code. Many nightclubs have strict dress codes, and offenders may be turned away at the door. It is also important to pace yourself when it comes to alcohol consumption and to be aware of your surroundings to preserve your safety.

Finally, remember that Ibiza has a rich cultural heritage that should be treasured and maintained. The island features a unique blend of influences, including Phoenician, Roman, and Moorish civilizations, as well as a rich history that should be explored and appreciated. When interacting with locals, it is important to respect their conventions and traditions while being open-minded and respectful.

Chapter 5: Transportation Options

There are several different modes of transportation in Ibiza for tourists to get around the island. In this guide, we will discuss the different modes of transportation in Ibiza, their prices, pros, and cons, to help tourists choose the best option for their needs.

Taxis

Taxis are one of the most common ways of transportation in Ibiza. They are affordable and convenient for getting to the island. Taxis are likewise relatively inexpensive, with short-distance costs starting at about €3.25 and averaging €10–€15.

One of the advantages of taking a taxi in Ibiza is that it is a quick and easy way to get around the island. There will be no need to search for parking or navigate unfamiliar roads. Furthermore, taxi drivers are typically locals who are familiar with the area and can offer helpful tips and recommendations for places to visit.

One disadvantage of taking a taxi in Ibiza is that long-distance fares can be quite expensive. Furthermore, during peak tourist season, finding a taxi can be difficult, especially late at night when people are heading out to the clubs.

Buses

Another popular mode of transportation in Ibiza is the bus. The island has a well-developed bus system that connects all of the major towns and tourist destinations. Bus tickets are reasonably priced, with single tickets costing between €2 and €3 and a 10-ride pass costing between €12 and €15.

One of the advantages of taking the bus in Ibiza is that it is a cost-effective way of getting around the island. Furthermore, buses are a great option for tourists who want to explore the island on their own because they allow them to get on and off at various stops along the way.

The bus schedules in Ibiza can be unreliable, especially during peak tourist season when buses can become overcrowded. Furthermore, because buses make frequent stops, they can be slow, especially when traveling long distances.

Car Rentals

Another popular mode of transportation for visitors to Ibiza is car rental. Several car rental agencies are located throughout the island and offer a wide variety of vehicles at reasonable prices. Prices for a small economy car in Ibiza begin at around €20 per day and rise depending on the type of vehicle and the length of the rental period.

One advantage of renting a car in Ibiza is the ability to explore the island at your own pace. You can create your itinerary and visit remote beaches and villages that are not accessible via public transportation. In addition, renting a vehicle is pretty cheap, especially if you are traveling with a group of friends or family.

One downside to hiring a vehicle in Ibiza is that the roads may be narrow and twisting, particularly in the island's rural sections. Furthermore, parking might be problematic, especially during the high tourist season when parking places are sparse.

Scooters/Motorbikes

Renting a scooter or motorcycle might be a terrific alternative for individuals searching for a more adventurous means of transportation. Scooters and motorbikes may be leased across the island for as little as €15 per day.

One perk of hiring a scooter or motorbike in Ibiza is that it is a fun and thrilling way to explore the island. Furthermore, scooters and motorbikes are relatively simple to park, and they might be an ideal method to escape traffic congestion that usually arises during peak tourist season.

One downside of hiring a scooter or motorbike in Ibiza is that it may be risky, especially for new riders. Ibiza's roadways may be busy and twisty, and riding a two-wheeled vehicle increases the chance of an accident. It's important to wear protective gear and exercise caution when riding.

Bicycles

For eco-conscious visitors who prefer cycling, renting a bicycle can be a superb transportation choice in Ibiza. Several rental shops offer bicycles, including mountain bikes and electric bikes, with prices starting at around €10 per day.

One of the pros of renting a bicycle in Ibiza is that it allows you to explore the island at a leisurely pace while enjoying the fresh air and beautiful scenery. Cycling is also a great way to stay active and eco-friendly during your visit.

One of the cons of renting a bicycle in Ibiza is that the island has hilly terrain, which can make cycling more challenging, especially for beginners or those not used to cycling uphill. Additionally, the roads in some areas may not have dedicated cycling lanes, so cyclists need to be cautious and share the road with other vehicles.

Walking

Ibiza is a fairly tiny island, and many of the main tourist sites are within walking distance of each other. Walking is a practical and cost-effective option to move around, especially if you are staying in a central neighborhood.

One of the pros of walking in Ibiza is that it allows you to thoroughly immerse yourself in the island's beauty and discover the tiny alleys and hidden locations that are inaccessible to motors. Walking also allows you to discover local shops, cafes, and landmarks at your own pace.

One of the cons of walking in Ibiza is that it may not be practical for longer distances or if you have limited time. While walking is a good option for short distances, it may not be realistic for reaching locations that are positioned far apart or in rural regions.

Chapter 6: Must-See Museums in Ibiza

I biza is well-known for its boisterous nightlife and stunning beaches, but it also boasts a vibrant cultural scene with a variety of fascinating museums to explore. If you are a history buff, an art enthusiast, or just curious about the island's past, these are the top seven must-see museums in Ibiza for tourists.

Archaeological Museum of Ibiza:

The Archaeological Museum of Ibiza, located in Dalt Vila's old town, is a treasure trove of prehistoric and Phoenician artifacts that shed light on the island's past. While viewing well-preserved pottery, tools, and sculptures, visitors may learn about the island's early people and their way of life. The museum also has an extraordinary collection of Punic and Roman artifacts that provide a complete picture of Ibiza's historical significance.

Puig des Molins Necropolis:

A trip to the Puig des Molins Necropolis is like going back in time. This huge Phoenician-era burial ground is a UNESCO World Heritage site and one of the Mediterranean's most important ancient necropolises. The museum has a huge collection of ancient tombs, sarcophagi, and funeral artifacts, which provide a unique glimpse into the island's burial practices and ceremonies.

Contemporary Art Museum of Ibiza:

For art lovers, the Contemporary Art Museum of Ibiza is a must-see. The museum, which is built in a former slaughterhouse, features a diverse collection of modern artworks by local and international artists. The museum's constantly changing shows include everything from paintings and sculptures to multimedia installations and experimental works, all of which represent Ibiza's dynamic and lively art culture.

Can Ros Cultural Center:

Can Ros Cultural Center, located in the picturesque town of Santa Eulalia, is an architectural marvel that showcases the island's cultural history. In the exhibition areas of this wonderfully restored 17th-century farmhouse, visitors may explore diverse art exhibitions, historical objects, and traditional handicrafts. The center also hosts cultural events, seminars, and concerts, providing visitors with a comprehensive understanding of Ibiza's traditions and customs.

Ethnographic Museum of Ibiza:

Learn about the island's agrarian history at the Ethnographic Museum of Ibiza in the lovely town of San Carlos. The museum, located in a typical Ibicenco farmhouse, offers an entire experience of island rural life. Visitors may learn about traditional farming procedures, handicrafts, and local customs by wandering through rooms filled with actual furniture, equipment, and agricultural goods.

Museum of Contemporary Art of Ibiza:

The Museum of Modern Art of Ibiza is a haven for art lovers, showcasing modern art in all of its forms. The museum, situated in the busy marine sector of Ibiza Town, features a collection of works by notable local and worldwide artists. The museum's modern masterwork collection includes everything from paintings and sculptures to photography and digital media.

Ses Païsses:

Discover the secrets of Ibiza's ancient towns at Ses Pases, an archaeological site near Santa Eulalia. This amazing Bronze Age village provides a rare glimpse into the island's past, with well-preserved elements such as defensive walls, dwellings, and even a sacred shrine. The site's museum contains extensive information on archaeological artifacts as well as the daily life of its occupants, making it an intriguing historical visit.

Festivals and celebrations in Ibiza

Ibiza offers a rich cultural experience through its festivals and celebrations. Tourists visiting Ibiza can immerse themselves in the local traditions and experience the island's unique culture. In this guide, we will explore some of the top festivals and celebrations in Ibiza.

Ibiza Carnival

Every February, the Ibiza Carnival, a vivid and colorful occasion, takes place. It honors the island's history, culture, and customs. Ibiza's streets come alive with dancing, music, and people wearing bright costumes during the carnival. Tourists get a fantastic chance to enjoy the colorful and dynamic environment of the island.

Flower Power

Every summer in Ibiza, there is an event called Flower Power. It honors the hippie culture of the island and the 1960s and 1970s period. People dress up like hippies and dance to vintage music throughout the event. The event is hosted in Pacha, one of the most well-known nightclubs on the island, and it is a must-see for visitors.

Medieval Festival

Every May, Dalt Vila, a walled town, hosts the Medieval Festival, a distinctive festival. The town is transformed into a medieval market for the duration of the festival, complete with jousting contests, medieval games, and street performances. It is a wonderful chance for visitors to learn about the history and culture of the island.

Eivissa Jazz Festival

Annually, in September, the Eivissa Jazz Festival takes place. Some of the top jazz performers from across the globe attend this festival of jazz music. Tourists get a wonderful chance to experience jazz music and the rich culture of the island during the event, which is held in Ibiza Town's historic center.

Ibiza Rocks.

San Antonio hosts the Ibiza Rocks music event every summer. Some of the top artists in the world come here to celebrate rock and alternative music. Tourists get the chance to enjoy fantastic music and take in the lively atmosphere of the island during the event, which is held at the Ibiza Rocks Hotel.

Fiestas de San Juan

Every June, Ibiza hosts the annual festival known as the Fiestas de San Juan. It is a summer solstice event that features bonfires, fireworks, and street gatherings. Tourists get a wonderful chance to engage in local celebrations and learn about the island's traditional culture.

Ibiza Gay Pride

Every June, the island's LGBTQ+ community gathers for the Ibiza Gay Pride Festival. A parade, block parties, and live entertainment are all part of it. It is a fantastic chance for guests to celebrate diversity and inclusiveness while enjoying the island's bustling vibe.

Nit de Sant Joan

The Nit de Sant Joan is a traditional ceremony that takes place in June in San Juan. It is a summer solstice event that features bonfires, fireworks, and street gatherings. Tourists get a wonderful chance to engage in local celebrations and learn about the island's traditional culture.

Ibiza Reggae Festival

The Ibiza Reggae Festival is a festival of reggae music and takes place every summer in San Antonio. It gathers some of the top reggae artists from across the globe and features live concerts, DJs, and street parties. It's a wonderful chance for visitors to take in the vibrant ambiance of the island while listening to fantastic music.

Sant Bartomeu Fiesta

Every August in San Antonio, there is a customary festival called the Sant Bartomeu Fiesta. It features parades, street festivities, and live entertainment in honor of the town's patron saint. Tourists get a wonderful chance to engage in local celebrations and learn about the island's traditional culture.

Ibiza International Film Festival

Every year in October, the Ibiza International Film Festival takes place. It draws filmmakers and movie fans from all around the globe as a celebration of independent film. The festival offers visitors a great chance to see the island's creative and cultural side and includes film screenings, seminars, and panel discussions.

Ibiza Yoga Festival

Every summer in Santa Eulalia, there is a festival honoring yoga and well-being called the Ibiza Yoga Festival. It features live music and performances, workshops, conferences, and yoga lessons. Tourists get a great chance to relax and rejuvenate while taking in the tranquil ambiance of the island.

Ibiza Food Festival

Every year in May, there is a festival called the Ibiza Food Festival. It features food tastings, cooking lessons, and seminars as a celebration of the island's culinary sector. The event, which takes place around the island, gives visitors a great chance to sample the regional cuisine and get a sense of the island's culinary traditions.

Ibiza Light Festival

Every December, there is the Ibiza Light Festival, a festival of light and art. Various venues throughout the island will host performances, projections, and light projects. Tourists get a wonderful chance to discover the artistic and creative side of the island while taking in the festive ambiance.

Best Beaches in Ibiza

Ibiza, Spain's third-largest Balearic Island, is a popular destination for beachgoers from all over the globe. The island is famous for its crystal blue seas, breathtaking shoreline, and laid-back vibe, making it an excellent place for both leisure and partying. With over 50 beaches to select from, it might be difficult to choose the best one. If you're planning a vacation to Ibiza, these are the top 15 greatest beaches you should visit.

Cala Comte

Cala Comte is a well-known beach for tourists who want to take in Ibiza's natural beauty. It is located on the western shore of the island.. Cala Comte is the perfect place to relax, soak up the sun, and go swimming in the Mediterranean Sea because of its clean waters and golden beach.

Playa d'en Bossa

One of Ibiza's longest beaches, Playa d'en Bossa is nearly three kilometers long. This beach is well-liked by partygoers because of its thriving nightlife, which has several pubs and clubs.

Cala Saladeta

On Ibiza's west coast, next to Cala Salada, lies a small, uninhabited beach called Cala Saladeta. Due to its turquoise waters and rocky outcrops, this beach is excellent for diving and snorkeling.

Cala Bassa

Another gorgeous beach on the west coast of Ibiza is Cala Bassa. Due to the shallow waters, families with children often visit this beach. The beach is a great area to spend the day since it also has a lot of dining and drinking options.

Talamanca

The well-liked beach of Talamanca is just a short drive from Ibiza Town. Talamanca is the perfect place to relax because of its calm waters and wide stretches of beach. The beach is a great place for lunch or a drink since it has so many pubs and restaurants.

Cala Jondal

A well-known beach on Ibiza's south coast is Cala Jondal. The beach is renowned for its crystal-clear waters and stunning surroundings. Cala Jondal is a great area to party since it has several beach clubs.

Es Cavallet

The southern coast of Ibiza has a lengthy sandy beach called Es Cavallet. The beach attracts many kites and windsurfers and is well-known for its stunning views. Es Cavallet is a great area to stop for lunch or a drink since it also has several beach bars.

Cala Xarraca

On Ibiza's north coast, there is a deserted beach called Cala Xarraca. The beach, which is surrounded by high cliffs, is a well-liked spot for diving and snorkeling. Cala Xarraca is a great place for lunch or a drink since it has so many pubs and restaurants.

Aguas Blancas

On Ibiza's east coast, there is a stunning beach called Aguas Blancas. High cliffs surround the beach, which boasts crystal-clear waters perfect for swimming. Due to the huge waves, Aguas Blancas is also a well-liked surfing location.

Cala Tarida

Popular beach Cala Tarida is located on the west coast of Ibiza. Due to its shallow seas, the beach is popular among families with young children. Cala Tarida is a great destination for a day trip since it also boasts a wide selection of eateries and pubs.

Benirras

The north coast of Ibiza has a stunning beach called Benirras. The beach, which is encircled by pine trees, is a well-liked location to see the setting sun. Benirras is a fantastic location for diving and snorkeling because of its clean waters and rocky outcrops.

Sa Caleta

The south coast of Ibiza has a stunning beach called Sa Caleta. The beach is a well-known fishing location and is recognized for its red rocks. There are many caverns and interesting rock formations to find at Sa Caleta, making it a fantastic place for exploration.

Cala Llonga

Popular beach Cala Llonga is located on Ibiza's east coast. The beach is a great spot to unwind and relax because of its tranquil waves. Cala Llonga is a nice place for lunch or a drink since it also includes a variety of eateries and pubs.

Es Figueral

On Ibiza's northeastern shore sits the tranquil beach of Es Figueral. The hills that surround the shore provide a wonderful walking environment. Es Figueral's crystal-clear seas and golden beaches make it a fantastic place for swimming and tanning.

Las Salinas

The south coast of Ibiza is home to the lovely beach of Las Salinas. The beach is a well-liked location for swimming and tanning since it is bordered by pine trees. Numerous beach clubs can be found in Las Salinas, making it a popular place to party.

Outdoor Activities

Ibiza is well-known for its dynamic nightlife and electronic music scene, but the island also has a variety of outdoor activities for visitors to enjoy. Ibiza provides something for everyone who wants to enjoy the great outdoors, from water sports to hiking and cycling. Here are the top 11 outdoor activities for visitors in Ibiza:

Snorkeling and scuba diving

Ibiza offers clear, blue waters that are great for snorkeling and diving. You may explore the underwater world and view a variety of marine life, including colorful fish, octopuses, and sea turtles. The waters around the island also include several interesting shipwrecks that provide an amazing diving experience.

Kayaking

Kayaking is a wonderful way to explore the island's coastline. Paddle through hidden coves and caves to discover secluded beaches and jaw-dropping rock formations. There are various kayaking trips available on the island, ranging from short outings to full-day expeditions.

SUP (Stand-Up Paddleboarding)

SUP, or stand-up paddleboarding, is a popular activity on the island of Ibiza. It's a fantastic chance to view the island's beaches and sparkling blue ocean. Paddle along the beach or amid the island's secluded coves and caves. SUP boards may be readily hired, and various SUP tours are available on the island.

Cliff Jumping

Cliff jumping is a thrilling activity for adrenaline junkies in Ibiza. There are many spots on the island where you can jump over cliffs into the crystal-clear oceans below. While cliff jumping is an amazing experience, it is not recommended for inexperienced swimmers or those who are afraid of heights.

Hiking

Ibiza has several hiking trails that provide stunning views of the island's natural beauty. The rugged coastline, lush woodlands, and rolling hills of the island may all be explored. There are various guided hiking programs offered on the island, ranging from easy hikes to more demanding climbs.

Cycling

Cycling is a fantastic way to experience the island's beauty and beaches. There are various nice cycling paths on the island, including the well-known Sa Caleta Circle. Renting a bike or joining a guided riding excursion allows you to explore the island at your leisure.

Horseback Riding

Horseback riding is a wonderful opportunity to see the island's natural splendor. Riding through the countryside provides views of vineyards, woods, and rolling hills. There are various horseback riding experiences available on the island for riders of all levels.

Yoga

Yoga is a common practice in Ibiza, an island known for its health spas. Many hotels and resorts offer yoga sessions, and many yoga studios offer drop-in classes. Yoga in Ibiza's natural surroundings is a tranquil experience that is a wonderful way to unwind and reconnect with nature.

Parasailing

Parasailing is a thrilling activity accessible in Ibiza for anyone seeking an adrenaline rush. Fly over the island's coastline for breathtaking views of its natural splendor. Many of the island's beaches provide parasailing.

Jet Skiing

Jet skiing is a popular hobby in Ibiza, and it's a great way to explore the island's coastline. Renting a jet ski allows you to explore the island's hidden coves and beaches. Jet skiing is accessible on several of the island's beaches, and there are many guided jet ski tours available.

Boat Tours

Exploring the island by boat is a common hobby in Ibiza. A boat tour around the island offers stunning views of the coastline and its hidden coves and beaches. Several boat trips are available, ranging from catamaran tours to speedboat tours. Certain itineraries may include snorkeling breaks and trips to secluded beaches. It's a terrific opportunity to see the island from a different perspective and admire its natural beauty.

Shopping in Ibiza

Ibiza, a beautiful Mediterranean Sea island, is renowned for its vibrant nightlife and stunning beaches. Nonetheless, it is a terrific shopping location. Ibiza has something for everyone, whether you want souvenirs, trendy clothing, or one-of-a-kind gifts.

Dalt Vila, Ibiza's historic town, is a fantastic shopping destination. This historic quarter is tightly filled with charming shops and art galleries. Handcrafted pottery and regionally made jewelry may be found here.

Las Dalias hippie market is another well-known shopping destination in Ibiza. This market, which has been open since the 1950s, is noted for its colorful booths and bohemian atmosphere. Everything from homemade clothing to organic food is available here.

If you want to purchase premium clothes, head to Marina Ibiza. This area is known for its high-end shopping, including stores such as Gucci and Prada. Local merchants may also sell one-of-a-kind products that you won't find anywhere else.

For a more traditional shopping experience, go to one of the island's many markets. The Mercado de Ibiza is great for fresh cuisine and local delicacies, while the Mercado Viejo is famous for antiques and vintage items.

Visit one of Ibiza's many shopping malls if you need some retail therapy. The Ibiza Gran Hotel Shopping Center is one of the largest on the island, with a varied range of businesses selling anything from luxury goods to technology.

Visit one of the island's many independent businesses if you're looking for something unique. La Galeria Elefante is a great example, offering a wide range of homeware, clothing, and accessories. El Rastro Ibiza also offers handmade leather goods and vintage clothing at Retro Gusto.

Without some souvenir purchases, no shopping visit to Ibiza would be complete. Visit one of the many gift shops on the island for anything from keychains to postcards. Alternatively, you may visit one of the island's many artisanal markets to find handmade handicrafts and gifts.

When it comes to food shopping, Ibiza offers plenty of options. There are various grocery shops on the island, like Eroski and Mercadona, where you can acquire anything you need. Several specialty food establishments sell anything from artisanal cheeses to organic vegetables.

If you're looking for something unique, why not try some of Ibiza's native delicacies? A spicy pork sausage called sobrasada is a must-try. Local cheeses are also available, such as mató, a smooth and creamy goat's milk cheese.

Prices in Ibiza may be rather pricey, especially in the more popular areas. If you're willing to go off the beaten path, you can find some excellent deals. Markets and small stores are often the best places to locate one-of-a-kind and moderately priced items.

Remember to respect the local customs and traditions while shopping in Ibiza. Many markets and local businesses are closed on Sundays, and it is essential to dress appropriately while visiting religious institutions such as churches.

Chapter 7: Ibiza Nightlife and Dining

I biza, known as the world's party capital, offers a nightlife experience unlike any other. The island is well-known for its vibrant club scene, stunning beach parties, and wide lineup of world-class DJs. Ibiza's charm extends beyond its nightlife, with a diverse gastronomy scene catering to all tastes and budgets. Ibiza's entertainment and dining options ensure that guests have an unforgettable experience.

When the sun sets in Ibiza, the island comes alive. This city's nightlife is well-known, attracting visitors from all over the globe. The main partying areas are Ibiza Town, San Antonio, and Playa d'en Bossa. These areas are tightly packed with a wide variety of clubs, each with its own particular vibe and music style. From the iconic Pacha to the underground ambiance of DC10 and the seaside splendor of Ushuaa, there is a club to suit every taste.

The partying in Ibiza does not stop at the clubs. The island is famous for its beach clubs and open-air celebrations. Café del Mar and Café Mambo, both situated along San Antonio's sunset strip, provide stunning views accompanied by chill-out music, making them excellent spots to have a drink while watching the sunset. Bora Bora and Nassau Beach Club in Playa d'en Bossa provide a more dynamic beachside experience, with well-known DJs playing the latest tunes.

Apart from the party scene, Ibiza boasts a diverse cuisine scene to suit all preferences. The island's dining options range from modest tapas bars to

Michelin-starred restaurants. Exploring Ibiza Town's narrow passageways reveals beautiful cafés serving traditional Spanish fare such as paella and fresh seafood. Traditional Ibicenco dishes like "Bullit de Peix" (fish stew) and "Sofrit Pagès" (beef and potato stew) are available to visitors.

Ibiza embraces global tastes as well, with restaurants providing cuisine from all over the world. From Italian trattorias to sushi eateries and Mexican cantinas, there's something for everyone. Many restaurants make use of the island's natural beauty, offering spectacular sea views and romantic settings. Visitors may enjoy a "dinner with a show" at one of Ibiza's renowned dinner clubs, where world-class entertainment is paired with outstanding cuisine for a unique experience.

It's hard to discuss the island's dining scene without noting the island's vibrant street food culture. The island's Las Dalias and Punta Arabi markets are well-known for their food merchants providing delightful nibbles and international goodies. Everything from Spanish churros and empanadas to Indian curries and Middle Eastern falafels is available to visitors. These markets provide a vibrant setting in which visitors may immerse themselves in local culture while enjoying a tasty meal.

To complement its nightlife and dining experiences, Ibiza boasts a profusion of pre-party activities. The island is equipped with gorgeous beaches, several of which host beach clubs that transform into nightclubs after the sun sets. Tourists may spend the day sunbathing on the lovely beaches, followed by a night of dancing under the stars. Ibiza also features breathtaking natural scenery, including the UNESCO-listed Dalt Vila and Es Vedrà. Exploring these sites throughout the day provides a peaceful contrast to the lively nightlife.

For those seeking a more relaxed vacation, Ibiza's gentler towns and villages offer excellent possibilities. For example, Santa Gertrudis is a beautiful village with wonderful cafés and art galleries. It provides a peaceful escape from the bustling party scene, allowing tourists to unwind and experience the island's distinct character. Similarly, the well-known hippy market Las Dalias is located in San Carlos, where travelers may peruse handmade handicrafts and jewelry while listening to live music and enjoying wonderful food.

Boat parties are another distinguishing feature of Ibiza's nightlife. Tourists may charter a private boat or join a group party to experience the island's stunning coastline while sipping cocktails and dancing to the beats of local DJs. These activities give an unforgettable experience as well as a chance to see Ibiza from a different perspective.

Ibiza's nightlife and dining options are affordable for all budgets, with a variety of options available. Visitors may enjoy a night out at one of the island's countless bars or a wonderful meal at a local tapas bar without breaking the bank. Alternatively, those seeking a more lavish experience may choose from a variety of high-end restaurants and clubs that provide VIP services and one-of-a-kind experiences.

Ibiza Foods

Ibiza is well-known for its vibrant nightlife, beautiful beaches, and stunning architecture, but it is also well-known for its unique and wonderful cuisine. The island's food reflects its history, geography, and influences from other cultures. Ibiza is a flavor, spice, and texture melting pot that you won't find anywhere else.

If you're thinking about visiting Ibiza, you should experience the island's food. Ibiza's food is light, healthy, and flavorful. Ibiza restaurants range from traditional Spanish tapas cafes to Michelin-starred gourmet dining establishments. Whatever your preferences are, there is something here for you.

The famous "sobrasada" is a must-try dish in Ibiza. This is a smoked sausage made from ground pork that has been seasoned with paprika. It's often spread over toast or used in cooking to provide a rich, smoky flavor to dishes. Another popular dish in Ibiza is "ensaimadas," which are delicious pastries made with wheat, sugar, eggs, and fat. They're often dusted with powdered sugar and filled with chocolate, cream, or other delicious fillings.

If you're looking for something a bit more substantial, go for the "bullit de peix." This traditional Ibicenco fish stew is made with various fish, potatoes, and saffron. Slow-cooking the stew for many hours enables the flavors to blend and create a rich, fragrant broth. It's frequently accompanied by rice and alioli, a garlicky mayonnaise-like sauce.

Seafood lovers might have the "calamari a la plancha," which is grilled squid seasoned with garlic, parsley, and olive oil. This dish is often served as a tapa, or small plate, and is great for sharing with friends over drinks.

For meat lovers, the "arroz de matanzas" is a must-try. Rice flavored with pig, fowl, and rabbit, as well as vegetables and saffron. It's a hearty, delicious dish that's perfect for a cold winter day.

If you're looking for something lighter, try the "ensalada payesa." This salad is popular in Ibiza and is made out of lettuce, tomato, onion, olives, and roasted peppers. It's usually served with bread and alioli.

The other popular dish in Ibiza is "paella." This rice dish originated in Valencia but has now grown popular across Spain, including Ibiza. Paella is a rice dish that is commonly seasoned with saffron and other spices and served with chicken, rabbit, or seafood. It's prepared in a large, shallow pan and served in family-style portions.

Ibiza's famous drinks

Ibiza is well-known for its stunning beaches, exciting nightlife, and refreshing cocktails. When it comes to beverages, Ibiza offers a vast selection to suit all preferences. There's something for everyone, from traditional Spanish beverages to inventive cocktails. As a visitor to Ibiza, you should be aware of the popular cocktails that you should taste throughout your trip.

The Hierbas Ibicencas is one of Ibiza's most well-known beverages. It's a traditional liqueur prepared from plants and spices native to the island. This drink has a peculiar taste that is both sweet and bitter, and it is often consumed after supper. Hierbas Ibicencas is a must-try if you want to try something traditional.

Sangria is another popular drink in Ibiza. This cool cocktail is created with red wine, chopped fruits, and sometimes brandy or triple sec. The fruit adds a sweet and tart taste to the sangria, making it ideal for a hot day at the beach. Sangria is available at practically every bar and restaurant in Ibiza, but it's usually better to ask the locals for their favorite.

Ibiza features a popular beverage called the Ibiza Ice for those seeking a little bit of a kick. This drink contains vodka, lemon juice, and Sprite. It's a cool cocktail that's ideal for a hot day, and the vodka adds a little additional bite. Ibiza Ice is one of the island's most popular drinks, so make sure to sample it.

If you want to try a traditional drink, the Mojito is a good option. This cocktail contains white rum, lime juice, soda water, and mint. It's a refreshing cocktail excellent for a night out, and you can get it at any bar in Ibiza. Mojitos are ideal for individuals who enjoy a simple but delicious beverage.

Try the Chupito if you're searching for something a bit different. Chupito is a shot of alcohol often served in a shot glass. It is available in many flavors, including chocolate, caramel, and strawberry. Chupitos is an excellent way to sample a range of tastes without committing to a whole drink.

Ibiza features a pleasant drink called Horchata for individuals who don't want to consume alcohol. This beverage contains pulverized almonds, water, and sugar. It has a nutty taste that is ideal for a hot day and is a favorite option among individuals who do not use alcohol.

Agua de Valencia is another popular non-alcoholic drink in Ibiza. This cocktail contains orange juice, cava, gin, and vodka. It's a refreshing drink that's ideal for individuals who dislike the taste of alcohol but yet want to have a good time. Agua de Valencia is a terrific way to enjoy Ibiza's nightlife without drinking alcohol.

Try the Absinthe Ritual for a one-of-a-kind experience. Absinthe is a green, anise-flavored spirit with high alcohol content. Pouring absinthe over a sugar cube and then lighting it on fire is the Absinthe Ritual. It's a dramatic way to drink and a one-of-a-kind experience that will be remembered.

The Hierbas con Hielo is a great option for those looking for a sweet treat. Hierbas Ibicencas, sugar, and ice are used to make this drink. It's a sweet drink ideal for those with a sweet tooth. Hierbas with Hielo is a famous beach drink that is a terrific way to cool down on a hot day in Ibiza.

The Jägerbomb is a popular drink in the Ibiza club scene. A shot of Jägermeister is mixed into a glass of Red Bull to make this drink. It's a high-energy drink that's ideal for folks who want to party all night. The Jägerbomb is a popular drink at many Ibiza nightclubs and is a must-try for everyone seeking a good time.

If you like gin, Ibiza offers a popular gin-based beverage called the Gin Fizz. Gin, lemon juice, sugar, and soda water are used to make this beverage. It's a cool drink that's ideal for a hot summer day. Gin Fizzes are a popular drink at beach bars and are an excellent way to cool down and relax.

The Sex on the Beach is a popular drink for those looking for something fruity and refreshing. This drink is constructed with vodka, peach schnapps, orange juice, and cranberry juice. It's a sweet and fruity drink that's excellent for a hot day at the beach. Sex on the Beach is a popular drink at beach bars and is a terrific way to cool down and relax.

For those searching for a distinctive drink, the Blue Lagoon is a popular option. This drink is constructed with vodka, blue curaçao, and lemonade. It's a vivid blue beverage with a sweet and sour taste that's ideal for a hot summer day. The Blue Lagoon is a popular beverage at beach bars and is a terrific way to cool down and enjoy the sun.

Another renowned drink in Ibiza is the Pina Colada. This drink is composed of rum, coconut cream, and pineapple juice. It's a sweet and creamy drink that's excellent for a hot day at the beach. Pina Coladas are a popular drink at beach bars and are an excellent way to calm down and relax.

If you like tequila, Ibiza offers a well-known tequila-based beverage called the Margarita. Tequila, lime juice, and triple sec are used to make this drink. It's a refreshing drink that's excellent for a hot day. Margaritas are a popular option at beach bars and are a terrific way to cool down and relax.

If you're searching for a one-of-a-kind experience, try the Green Beast, an absinthe-based drink popular in Ibiza. This drink contains absinthe, lemon juice, sugar, and soda water. It has a vivid green hue and a distinct taste that is ideal for individuals searching for something new. The Green Beast is a popular option in Ibiza's pubs and clubs and is a must-try for anyone looking for a one-of-a-kind experience.

Top Cafés and Restaurants in Ibiza

Ibiza is one of Spain's most popular tourist destinations. With its stunning beaches, vibrant nightlife, and rich history, it's no wonder that so many people visit this island paradise each year. Apart from the parties and sunsets, Ibiza is home to some of the best cafés and restaurants in the region. In this piece, we'll look at the top cafés and restaurants in Ibiza, as well as why you should go there.

The first on our list is Passion Café. This café, which has many locations around the island, is a must see for anybody looking for a healthy and delicious meal. Passion Café employs fresh, organic ingredients that will satisfy even the most discerning palates. This café caters to all tastes, whether you want a quick breakfast or a leisurely lunch.

Wild beets are another wonderful healthy eating option. Wild Beets is an all-vegan restaurant in Santa Gertrudis that offers a unique and wonderful dining experience. This restaurant is excellent for anybody looking for a healthy and delicious meal, offering anything from colorful smoothie bowls to hearty salads and sandwiches.

Go to La Paloma if you want something a bit more extravagant. This restaurant in the lovely village of San Lorenzo serves traditional Spanish dishes with a modern twist. La Paloma, which specializes in fresh, locally made food, is excellent for a leisurely lunch or dinner with friends and family.

Visit Es Torrent for an authentic Ibiza experience. This seafood restaurant is close to the beach and provides stunning views of the Mediterranean as you dine. From grilled octopus to fresh fish and shellfish, Es Torrent has some of the best seafood on the island.

Go to Cova Santa if you want something a bit more upscale. This restaurant and nightclub is nestled in a beautiful cave and provides an unforgettable dining experience. Cova Santa is the perfect setting for a special occasion or a romantic night for two, with a focus on Mediterranean food and an unequaled wine collection.

Amante is another great option for upscale dining. This restaurant in Cala Llonga offers breathtaking views of the sea as you dine. Amante, which specializes in Mediterranean cuisine and has an extensive wine list, is great for a romantic dinner or a night out with friends.

Pikes provides a more laid-back dining experience. This iconic hotel and restaurant in the heart of Ibiza dates back to the 1970s. Pikes, with its focus on Mediterranean cuisine and relaxed atmosphere, is great for a leisurely lunch or dinner with friends.

Go to Bambuddha if you're searching for something a bit more exotic. In the heart of the island, this Asian-inspired restaurant offers a unique and flavorful dining experience. Bambuddha is the best place to explore Far Eastern cuisine, from sushi to noodle dishes and all in between.

Finally, no trip to Ibiza is complete until you visit Can Pilot. This traditional Spanish restaurant in San Rafael serves some of the island's best meat dishes. Can Pilot is an excellent choice for hearty and flavorful dishes ranging from grilled steaks to tender lamb chops?

Ibiza Dining Manner

The local cuisine is one of the things not to miss while visiting Ibiza. Visitors should, however, keep in mind that specific dining etiquette must be followed to have a pleasant dining experience. In this essay, we will look at the Ibiza dining scene for tourists.

To begin, it is essential to understand that Ibiza is known for its relaxed and tranquil demeanor. This suggests that the dining experience will be more casual than in other parts of Europe. It is, nevertheless, still vital to dress appropriately for the occasion. When dining out, smart-casual attire is recommended.

It is customary to wait for the host or hostess to seat you while entering a restaurant. It is also important to understand that requesting a specific table or seat is considered impolite since the host or hostess will usually assign you to a table based on availability and group size.

While ordering food, it is customary for the waiter or waitress to suggest meals or specials. It is frequently OK to ask for recommendations, especially if you are unfamiliar with the local cuisine. However, it is important to understand that tipping is not mandatory in Ibiza, but it is always appreciated. A tip of 5-10% is normally fair, however, bear in mind that certain restaurants may charge a service fee on top of the bill.

Wait until everyone at the table has been served before starting to eat when the dinner arrives. This demonstrates respect and allows everyone to begin eating together. It is also vital to use utensils while eating since it is not customary to eat with your hands unless the dish requires it.

When dining in Ibiza, remember the concept of "sobremesa." Sobremesa is a Spanish term that refers to the time spent at the table after a meal, mainly for socializing and enjoying each other's company. Because sobremesa is popular with Ibizan clients, it is important not to rush out of the restaurant after supper.

Another important aspect of Ibiza's eating etiquette is the choice of words. While Spanish is the official language of the island, many residents also speak English. Learning a few basic Spanish phrases, such as "por favor" (please) and "gracias" (thank you), is still important as a sign of respect for the local culture.

When it comes to drinking, Ibiza is well-known for its nightlife and party scene. It's important to note, though, that excessive drinking and noisy behavior in public places are not tolerated in Ibiza. When dining out, it is customary to order a drink with your meal, such as wine or beer. However, it is essential to drink responsibly and avoid being too drunk, since this may be considered impolite by the locals.

When paying the bill, it is customary to establish eye contact with the waiter or waitress and signal with your hand. It is also worth mentioning that, rather than each person paying for their lunch, it is typical for the group to split the bill equally. If there are any disagreements or misunderstandings, it is vital to communicate with the waiter or waitress to resolve the problem.

Chapter 8: Family Travel in Ibiza

The Spanish island of Ibiza is noted for its nightlife, parties, and electronic music culture. It does, however, have a lot to offer families looking for a more relaxing vacation. Family holidays in Ibiza may be a fantastic way to bond with loved ones, create lasting memories, and enjoy the natural beauty of the island.

One of Ibiza's most notable characteristics is its beaches. The island has over 50 beaches, each with its own unique traits and attractions. Some beaches are great for swimming, sunbathing, and water sports, but others are more tranquil and remote. Three of Ibiza's most popular family-friendly beaches include Cala Llonga, Santa Eulalia, and Cala San Vicente.

Cala Llonga is a beautiful beach that is great for families with children. Because the water is shallow and peaceful, children can swim and play safely. There are also some nearby restaurants and cafés where you can dine or drink while resting on the beach.

Santa Eulalia is another wonderful family-friendly beach in Ibiza. It has a long stretch of golden sand, a lovely sea, and several beach amenities such as sun loungers, parasols, and showers. There are various restaurants and taverns along the seafront, making it easy to obtain something to eat or drink.

Cala San Vicente is a rural beach perfect for families wishing to get away from the crowds. It is surrounded by cliffs and offers spectacular views of the sea. The beach is small but well-equipped, complete with sun loungers, parasols, and a beach bar.

Aside from the beaches, Ibiza offers a variety of family-friendly activities and attractions. One of the most popular activities is a boat tour of the island. This is an excellent chance to see Ibiza from a different perspective, find hidden coves and beaches, and enjoy the beautiful blue ocean.

Another enjoyable family activity in Ibiza is a trip to the Es Canar Hippy Market. Every Wednesday, this market is a great place to buy souvenirs, apparel, and jewelry. There is also live music, food sellers, and children's entertainment, making it an ideal family outing.

For families interested in history and culture, Ibiza has a profusion of museums and landmarks. The Dalt Vila, or the old town of Ibiza, is one of the island's most well-known landmarks. It is a UNESCO World Heritage Site with beautiful sea views and historic structures.

Other museums in Ibiza worth seeing include the Archaeological Museum of Ibiza and Formentera, which displays the island's rich history and cultural past. There's also the Ibiza Ethnographic Museum, which gives visitors a glimpse into the island's agricultural heritage.

Ibiza has a lot to offer in terms of family accommodation. Children's families may stay in a range of hotels, resorts, and apartments. Many of these accommodations provide swimming pools, kids' clubs, and kid-friendly activities, making them an excellent choice for families wishing to unwind and enjoy their vacation.

For families who want to be close to nature, there are many campsites and glamping sites on the island. These are fantastic options for families who want to spend time in nature and have a more rustic experience.

In terms of dining, Ibiza has a wealth of family-friendly options. Traditional Spanish cuisine, as well as other options such as Italian, Japanese, and Mexican, are available in plenty. Some seafood restaurants in Ibiza are a must-try. Because the island is surrounded by the Mediterranean Sea, fresh seafood is plentiful. Grilled octopus, paella, and fresh fish are among Ibiza's most popular seafood dishes.

The best kid's activities in Ibiza

Ibiza offers a wide range of family-friendly activities for children of all ages. From seeing the island's natural beauty to learning about its history and culture, there is something for everyone.

One of the best ways to enjoy the island with children is to spend time at one of the island's many beaches. Ibiza is well-known for its clear oceans and sandy beaches, and there are numerous child-friendly beaches. Cala Bassa is a popular choice for families because of its modest waters and smooth beach. Another great option is Playa d'en Bossa, which has a long stretch of beach and a variety of water sports.

For a more adventurous experience, take the family on a guided tour of the island's coastlines and hidden coves. The excursions may run anything from a few hours to a whole day, and some even include snorkeling or paddleboarding. It's a fantastic chance to see the island from a different perspective and create amazing moments with your family.

If your children are animal lovers, a visit to Ibiza's Aquarium Cap Blanc is a must. This one-of-a-kind aquarium is built within a natural cave and is home to a diverse array of marine life, including sharks, rays, and sea turtles. Children may learn about the many species and even touch and feed some of them.

For a more cultural experience, take the family to Dalt Vila, Ibiza's historic village. The narrow passageways and historic buildings provide a glimpse into the island's history, and youngsters may learn about it via guided tours or solo discovery. The views from the top of the town are especially beautiful, making it a great site for family photographs.

A visit to the Museum of Contemporary Art (MACE) is a necessity if your youngsters are interested in art. The museum is located in the old town and showcases modern art by local and international artists. Children may learn about different art styles and processes as well as participate in hands-on workshops.

For a more energetic experience, take the family on a hike to Sa Talaia, the island's highest point. The hike is arduous but rewarding, with breathtaking views of the island from the summit. Children may learn about the flora and fauna of the island while enjoying some fresh air and exercise.

Another delightful activity for youngsters in Ibiza is visiting the island's hippie markets. Throughout the week, markets in several towns and villages sell a variety of handmade goods, clothing, and jewelry. Children may explore the booths and even try their hand at bargaining with the shopkeepers.

Finally, no vacation to Ibiza is complete without a visit to Es Vedra, the famous rock formation off the island's coast. According to folklore, the rock has magical powers, and many people regard it as one of the world's most potent energy sites. While soaking in the beauty from the adjoining cliffs, children may learn about the traditions and mythology surrounding the rock.

Practical Tips for Traveling with Kids

Traveling with children may be a difficult experience for parents. It may, however, be a joyful and thrilling journey with proper planning and preparation. Here are some helpful hints for making traveling with children more enjoyable:

- Make a plan: It is critical to organize your journey ahead of time. Make a list of the things you wish to do, then research your location and book your accommodations. This will prevent any last-minute surprises and ensure that everything is in order before you go.
- Pack wisely: Less is more when it comes to packing. Pack just the necessities and leave the rest at home. Make sure your youngster has adequate clothing, diapers, wipes, and other basics. To keep your youngster amused throughout the ride, bring a small backpack with toys, books, and snacks.
- Take into account the time of day: If at all feasible, organize your flights or road excursions around your child's nap or bedtime. This will allow them to sleep for most of the voyage, allowing you to travel without disturbances.
- Bring a stroller or a child carrier: When traveling with children, bringing a stroller or carrier may be a lifesaver. It will help you to take your youngster throughout the airport or city without constantly carrying them.
- Keep your child entertained: Traveling may be tedious for children, therefore it is important to keep them amused. Toys, coloring books, and games may be brought along to keep children entertained throughout the travel. You may also keep your children engaged during lengthy trips by downloading movies or TV episodes on your tablet or phone.
- Be prepared for emergencies: It is important to be prepared for any emergency that may occur throughout your journey. Bring a first-aid kit, additional medicine, and any other materials you may need in case your kid becomes ill or injured.
- Be adaptable: It is important to be adaptable while traveling with children.It's okay if things don't go according to plan.. Be prepared to adapt your plans and adjust your schedule to meet the requirements of your kid if required.
- Take a break: It is essential to take stops and stretch your legs while driving long distances. You may make a pit stop or visit a park to let your toddler run about and burn off some energy. This will also provide you

with an opportunity to relax and refuel before continuing your adventure.

- Use technology to your advantage: When traveling with children, technology may be a valuable asset. Apps may help you identify family-friendly restaurants and activities, and GPS can help you navigate a new place. Stay in contact with family and friends back home by using video chat applications.

- Have some fun: Above all, remember to enjoy yourself! Traveling with children may be challenging, but it can also be a rewarding experience. Take the opportunity to relax and make memorable memories with your family.

Chapter 9: Mistakes Tourists to Avoid in Ibiza

I biza has its share of pitfalls and traps that unwary visitors might fall into. In this guide, we will highlight the top eight blunders that travelers should avoid while visiting Ibiza.

Overpacking

Overpacking is one of the most frequent errors travelers make while visiting Ibiza. Ibiza is a tiny island, so you won't need to carry much with you. Packing too much might be unpleasant when you need to relocate, and it can also be costly if you have to pay additional baggage costs. Furthermore, since Ibiza is a laid-back resort, formal attire is not required. Pack light, comfortable clothing that is appropriate for both the beach and the nightlife.

Ignorance of Local Culture

Ibiza has a distinct culture that must be respected. The natives are polite and friendly, yet they also have their own way of living. The Spanish siesta, for example, is a long-standing custom in Ibiza. Many stores and companies shut for a few hours in the afternoon, so schedule your activities accordingly. Additionally, while visiting holy locations, dress correctly and avoid loud and rude conduct.

Failure to Plan Ahead

Ibiza is a popular vacation destination, so make sure you plan ahead of time. Reservations are required at many restaurants and clubs, particularly during high season. If you don't plan, you can miss out on some of the greatest experiences on the island. It is also critical to arrange your accommodations ahead of time to prevent disappointment.

Too Much Money Spent

Ibiza is an expensive vacation that is easy to splurge on. Many travelers make the mistake of spending too much money on fancy restaurants and clubs, which may rapidly mount up. Instead, look for local restaurants and pubs with reasonable costs. Consider going to Ibiza during the off-season, when rates are cheaper. You may still enjoy the beauty and nightlife of the island without breaking the budget.

Neglecting Safety

Ibiza is typically a secure place, however taking care to protect yourself and your things is necessary. Don't leave valuables unattended on the beach, and keep an eye out for pickpockets in busy places. It's also crucial to drink sensibly and avoid bingeing on alcohol. Finally, be careful while out at night, particularly in unknown locations.

Heat Underestimation

Ibiza lies on the Mediterranean, and the summers may be brutal. Many visitors misjudge the heat and fail to take adequate measures, resulting in sunburn and dehydration. When spending time at the beach, it's important to apply sunscreen and drink lots of water. Also, try not to spend too much time in the sun during the warmest hours of the day.

Excessive use of alcohol and drugs

Ibiza is famous for its nightlife and party culture, however, excessive drinking and drug use may be risky and have significant effects. Many visitors fall victim to binge drinking and drug usage, which may result in accidents, injuries, and even death. It's important to drink responsibly and stay away from illicit drugs. Keep in mind that drink and drugs may affect your judgment and make you more susceptible to crime and accidents.

Not Exploring the Island

Finally, many people make the error of not venturing beyond the major party areas on the island. Ibiza has a rich history and culture to uncover, as well as many beautiful and calm areas. Explore the island's secret beaches, little towns, and gorgeous countryside by vehicle or bike. You'll be astounded by what you discover.

Tips for Saving Time, Money, and Stress

If not carefully planned, a vacation to Ibiza may rapidly become costly, time-consuming, and unpleasant. As a result, in this guide, we will advise on how to save time, money, and worry when visiting Ibiza.

Make a Plan

To save time, money, and worry in Ibiza, the first step is to prepare ahead of time. Research and book flights, lodging, and activities ahead of time to obtain the best discounts and avoid the last-minute rush. Check the weather forecast and prepare seasonally suitable clothing. Ibiza may be rather hot, so pack light clothes and sunscreen.

Selecting Your Accommodation Wisely

When traveling, one of the major costs is lodging. There are, however, numerous inexpensive choices in Ibiza, such as hostels, flats, and guesthouses. Look for accommodations near public transit to save money on taxis or vehicle rentals. To guarantee a more peaceful visit, try choosing accommodations in calmer places away from popular and loud tourist attractions.

Make use of public transportation.

Renting a vehicle in Ibiza may be costly, and finding parking can be difficult, particularly in the city center. As a result, it's best to make use of public transit, such as buses, which are both efficient and inexpensive. You may also hire a bike or scooter to explore the island at your leisure.

Go to Free Attractions

You may enjoy several free attractions in Ibiza, such as beaches, parks, and walking routes. Take advantage of the free outdoor places accessible on the island, which is noted for its natural beauty. You may also attend free activities such as concerts and festivals that take place regularly throughout the summer months.

Avoid Expensive Restaurants

Eating out in Ibiza may be costly, particularly in popular tourist locations. As a result, it's best to avoid pricey restaurants and instead seek out small cafes that provide reasonable meals. You may also save money by preparing meals at your lodging, particularly if it includes a kitchenette.

Carry Your Water

Water is vital, particularly during Ibiza's sweltering summer months. Purchasing bottled water, on the other hand, might be costly and wasteful. As a result, it's a good idea to bring your reusable water bottle and refill it at public fountains or your lodging.

Negotiate with street vendors

Street vendors are popular in Ibiza, particularly in tourist areas, and they may be aggressive while selling their wares. You may, however, save money by haggling with them. Always begin with a modest offer and work your way up to a price that is fair to both sides.

Avoid the High Season.

Ibiza's summer season runs from June to September when costs are at their greatest and the island is overrun with visitors. Consider visiting Ibiza during the low season, which runs from October to May, if you want to save money and avoid crowds. Although the weather is not as pleasant, you may still appreciate the island's natural beauty and the rates are substantially cheaper.

Plan your activities ahead of time.

If you want to participate in activities such as boat trips, water sports, or nightlife, it is best to schedule them in advance. This not only saves you money, but it also assures that you do not miss out on popular activities since they are in great demand. Furthermore, scheduling ahead of time helps you to organize your schedule and avoid spending time figuring out what to do next.

Learn the Fundamentals of Spanish

While many people in Ibiza speak English, knowing a few basic Spanish words will help you communicate with locals and navigate the island. It demonstrates that you are making an effort to understand and respect their culture, and they are more likely to be helpful and accommodating as a result. Before your travels, try language study applications like Duolingo or Babbel to acquire fundamental Spanish phrases.

Make Use of Discount Cards

Consider obtaining discount cards or package deals if you intend to visit many sites or participate in multiple activities. The Ibiza Card, for example, provides discounts on a variety of activities and services, such as clubs, restaurants, and vehicle rentals.

Avoid Paying ATM Fees

Using ATMs in Ibiza may be expensive, particularly if your bank charges foreign transaction fees. As a result, it's best to withdraw a large sum of money once and spend it during your vacation. To save on transaction costs, seek out banks that have relationships with your bank.

Itinerary Suggestions

If you're planning a vacation to Ibiza, there are so many things to see and do that it might be difficult to create an itinerary, but there are a few things you should keep in mind. Here are some ideas to help you arrange your ideal Ibiza holiday.

Day 1: Discover Ibiza Town

Ibiza Town is the island's capital and a perfect site to begin your journey.

Begin by touring the UNESCO World Heritage Site of the old town. The town's tiny alleyways and whitewashed houses give it a pleasant and distinct character. The Dalt Vila, a 16th-century fortification, is the main attraction of the old town. From the fortress's vantage point, you can see the whole town and the surrounding countryside. You may even go within the castle walls to see the Cathedral of Our Lady of the Snows.

Day 2: Go to Es Vedra.

Es Vedra is a tiny island off the shore of Ibiza's southwest coast. This rocky island is cloaked in folklore and mythology, and it is claimed to be one of the most magnetic spots on the planet. To explore Es Vedra up close, take a boat excursion from San Antonio or trek to the summit of Sa Pedrera, which gives beautiful views of the island and surrounding region.

Day 3: Unwind on the Beach

Ibiza is well-known for its stunning beaches, and there are several to pick from. Playa d'en Bossa, situated on the island's southern shore, is one of the most popular beaches. This large, sandy beach is ideal for swimming and sunbathing. Cala Comte, situated on the island's western shore, is another excellent alternative. This beach has pristine water and beautiful views of the adjacent islands.

Day 4: Visit Formentera for the Day

A little island called Formentera is located near Ibiza. It is well-known for its gorgeous beaches and crystal-clear water, making it a popular day trip destination from Ibiza. You may spend the day touring Formentera by taking a boat from Ibiza Town. Formentera's notable attractions are the Ses Illetes beach, which is regarded as one of the greatest beaches in Europe, and the Far de la Mola, a lighthouse situated on the island's southern edge.

Day 5: Enjoy Ibiza's Nightlife

Ibiza is famed for its nightlife, and no visit to the island is complete until you partake in it. There are several possibilities, including world-famous nightclubs like Pacha and Amnesia. If you want a more low-key experience, several pubs and restaurants provide live music and entertainment.

Day 6: Visit the Hippy Markets

Ibiza has a long history of hippy culture, and the island includes various markets that represent this. Las Dalias, situated in San Carlos, is the most well-known market. This market is open on Saturdays and sells a variety of items such as apparel, jewelry, and art. Punta Arabi, situated in the village of Es Canar, is another renowned market. This market is open on Wednesdays and has a similar selection of goods.

Day 7: Go Hiking

Ibiza is more than simply beaches and partying; it also boasts some breath-taking natural areas worth visiting. Hiking is one of the finest methods to do this. The Sa Talaia trek, which takes you to the highest point on the island, is one of the most popular. The trek is around 6 kilometers long and takes approximately 2-3 hours to complete. A stunning panoramic view of the island may be seen at the peak. The Atlantis trek, which brings you to a secret cove accessible only by foot, is another excellent alternative. The trek is around 3 kilometers long and takes approximately 1-2 hours to complete.

Day 8: Visit Sant Antoni de Portmany

Sant Antoni de Portmany is a town on Ibiza's western coast. It is well-known for its stunning sunsets and vibrant nightlife. Begin your vacation by strolling around the town's historic center, which is home to several taverns, restaurants, and stores. The Sunset Strip, a group of pubs and restaurants with spectacular views of the sunset, is one of Sant Antoni de Portmany's greatest attractions.

Day 9: Explore the Caves of the Island

There are some spectacular caverns in Ibiza that are worth investigating. The Cova de Can Marca, situated on the island's northern shore, is one of the most visited caves. The cave is around 100,000 years old and is rich in stalactites and stalagmites. The Cova de s'Argentera, situated in the village of Sant Mateu d'Albarca, is another excellent alternative. This cave has multiple ancient paintings and is one of the most significant archaeological sites on the island.

Day 10: Try Some Local Cuisine

A vacation to Ibiza would be incomplete without sampling some of the local food. The bullit de peix, a fish stew generally cooked with grouper and eaten with rice, is one of the island's most renowned meals. Sofrit pagès, a meat and vegetable stew often cooked with chicken, pig, and potatoes, is another popular meal. For dessert, have the flaó, a sweet and creamy cheesecake made with goat cheese and scented with aniseed.

FAQ

If you are planning a visit to Ibiza, you may have some questions. Here are some commonly asked questions and their answers to help you plan your vacation.

Q: When is the ideal time to visit Ibiza?

A: The best time to visit Ibiza is between May and October when the weather is nice and sunny. The main tourist season is from July through August, but you may still enjoy the island's beauty and activities in the shoulder seasons of May-June and September-October. The island tends to be quieter in the winter months, with many facilities shuttered.

Q: What is the best method to travel to Ibiza?

A: The simplest method to go to Ibiza is via aircraft. Ibiza Airport is well-connected to several major European cities, with direct flights from London, Paris, Amsterdam, and more. Alternatively, you may take a ferry from the Spanish mainland or surrounding islands.

Q: What are the greatest beaches in Ibiza?

A: Ibiza has over 80 beaches to choose from, each with its unique charm. Some of the best beaches in Ibiza are Cala Comte, Ses Salines, Cala d'Hort, and Cala Bassa. Cala Comte is known for its crystal-clear waters and stunning sunsets, while Ses Salines is popular for its lively atmosphere and beach clubs. Cala d'Hort offers views of the mystical Es Vedra rock formation, and Cala Bassa is great for families with children.

Q: How is the nightlife in Ibiza?

A: Ibiza is recognized for its dynamic nightlife, which includes world-famous clubs such as Pacha, Amnesia, and Ushuaia. These clubs attract world-class DJs and provide an unforgettable party experience. However, Ibiza's nightlife scene is not limited to clubs. There are also taverns, beach clubs, and restaurants with a vibrant environment.

Q: What are the best activities in Ibiza?

A: There is something for everyone in Ibiza. Ibiza has it all, whether you want a relaxing beach vacation or an action-packed adventure. The UNESCO World Heritage site of Dalt Vila, exploring the island's stunning beaches, hiking or cycling through the countryside, and enjoying the island's vibrant nightlife are just a few of the top things to do in Ibiza.

Q: Is Ibiza an expensive destination?

A: Ibiza can be an expensive destination, especially during the peak tourist season. However, there are ways to save money, such as staying in budget-friendly accommodations, eating at local restaurants, and avoiding the most popular tourist spots. If you plan your trip and budget accordingly, you can still have a fantastic time in Ibiza without breaking the bank.

Q: How is the food in Ibiza?

A: Ibiza's culinary scene is diverse, with influences from both Spanish and Mediterranean cuisine. Some of the local specialties to try include "bullit de peix," a fish stew, and "flaó," a sweet pastry made with cheese and aniseed. You can also find international cuisine in Ibiza, with many restaurants offering vegetarian and vegan options.

Q: What are the best areas to stay in Ibiza?

A: The best areas to stay in Ibiza depend on your preferences. If you are looking for a lively nightlife scene, you may want to stay in San Antonio or Playa d'en Bossa. For a more easygoing ambiance, try vacationing in Santa Eulalia or Cala Llonga. If you wish to be near the beach, you may stay at Talamanca, Figueretas, or Cala Llenya. Ibiza Town is also a popular place to stay in, with many choices for eating and shopping, as well as convenient access to the island's historical monuments.

Q: What is the culture like in Ibiza?

A: Ibiza has a distinct culture that has been shaped by its history and location. Since ancient times, the island has been inhabited, and its architecture represents the different civilizations that have resided there. Ibiza is also famous for its bohemian and hippie cultures, which flourished in the 1960s and 1970s. The island now draws a varied range of people, from partygoers to families, and the culture reflects this.

Q: Which day excursions from Ibiza are the best?

A: Ibiza is well-located for day visits to nearby islands and cities. Some of the greatest day adventures from Ibiza include visiting the neighboring island of Formentera, famed for its clean beaches and clear seas, touring the quaint village of Santa Gertrudis, or taking a boat journey to the nearby island of Es Vedra, known for its mysterious rock formations.

Q: What is the language spoken in Ibiza?

A: The official language of Ibiza is Spanish, although many inhabitants also speak Catalan, a regional language spoken in Catalonia, Valencia, and the Balearic Islands. English is also frequently spoken in the tourist regions, so you should not have any problem interacting.

Q: Are there any cultural events in Ibiza?

A: Ibiza boasts a thriving cultural scene, with various events throughout the year. In the warmer months, you may enjoy music events such as the Ibiza Rocks Festival or the International Music Summit. There are also art exhibits, cultural events, and gastronomic festivals throughout the year.

Q: What is the dress code like in Ibiza?

A: Ibiza has a loose and informal environment, and you may wear shorts and flip-flops to most locations. However, if you plan to go to a club or a high-end restaurant, you may want to dress up a bit. It is always a good idea to bring a light jacket or sweater for the evenings, as it can get chilly.

Q: Is Ibiza safe for tourists?

A: Ibiza is typically a safe place for travelers. However, like with any tourist location, you should take steps to keep your valuables secure and be cautious of your surroundings, particularly in busy places. It is likewise advisable to avoid wandering alone at night and instead employ certified cabs.

Conclusion

In conclusion, the Ibiza travel guide has presented a thorough description of this lovely island's culture, history, and tourist attractions. Ibiza offers something for everyone, from its beautiful beaches to its vibrant nightlife. The book has emphasized the different activities and events that take place throughout the year, making it an excellent summer and winter holiday location.

The guide also investigated the local food, which is a combination of Mediterranean and Spanish cuisines, and made suggestions for the finest places to visit. The tour also covers the architecture of the island, especially the famed Ibiza town and its historic sites.

One of Ibiza's most notable aspects is its thriving nightlife, which has been extensively covered in this book. The island is well-known for its well-known clubs and DJs, which draw partygoers from all over the globe. The book, however, has also emphasized the island's alternative sector, with a variety of smaller pubs and music venues catering to a wide clientele.

The book has selected numerous calm and attractive places to explore away from the throng for those looking for a more laid-back experience. In addition, the brochure describes the many outdoor activities available on the island, such as hiking and cycling.

Printed by Amazon Italia Logistica S.r.l.
Torrazza Piemonte (TO), Italy

57103804R00067